THE BIBLE JESUS LOVED

A Reasoned Way
to
Study the Old Testament

by

SAM WELLMAN

WILD CENTURIES PRESS

WILD CENTURIES PRESS
www.wildcenturies.com

ISBN-10: 0983584524
ISBN-13: 978-0-9835845-2-0

Typeface: Book Antiqua, Gill Sans MT

CONTENTS

PREFACE

Many think C.S. Lewis was the greatest Christian apologist of the 20th Century for the English-speaking world. This writer agrees with that opinion. What Lewis writes must be weighed with care. Although he was a renowned scholar he nevertheless wrote of things in which he was not a formal scholar, bringing his great intellect and wisdom to an issue. In that vein this writer--though with considerably less intellect and not one glimmer of wisdom--invokes the 'concession' of Lewis from page 1 of his 1958 work *Reflections on the Psalms*.

> This is not a work of scholarship. I am no Hebraist, no higher critic, no ancient historian, no archaeologist. I write for the unlearned about things in which I am unlearned myself.

C.S. Lewis essentially said he could be helpful to a fellow student "because he knows less" than an expert. Instead of knowing more and more about less and less, Lewis could still see the forest and help a fellow student see the forest too.

In the same vein this writer hopes *The Bible Jesus Loved* will be helpful to fellow Christians wanting to study the Bible, especially the daunting obligation of the Old Testament.

< I >

AMAZING FACTS ABOUT THE BIBLE JESUS LOVED

In the synagogue of his quiet village of Nazareth a young carpenter gazed upon the scroll of the prophet Isaiah and read:

> The Spirit of the Lord is on me, because he has anointed me to preach good news to the poor.
> He has sent me to proclaim freedom for the prisoners and recovery of sight for the blind, to release the oppressed, to proclaim the year of the Lord's favor.
> (Luke 4:18–19 NIV)[1]

The young carpenter then rolled up the scroll and announced, "Today this scripture is fulfilled in your hearing." (Luke 4:21)

The carpenter of course was Jesus. Yes, Jesus had just proclaimed to the Jews of Nazareth he was the Messiah prophesied by Isaiah in their Holy Scriptures. This great event in Nazareth is recorded in the fourth chapter of the book of Luke. It is perhaps the most electrifying example in the New Testament of Jesus quoting scriptures from the Jewish Holy Scriptures. The Holy Scriptures of the Jews is what is now also the Old Testament of Christians.[2]

And Jesus quoted the Old Testament often. It is an amazing fact that in the New Testament Jesus directly quoted Old Testament passages more than 40 times. In addition, Jesus mentioned by name the Old Testament notables Abel, Noah, Jonah, Lot, Abraham, Isaac, Jacob, Moses, Elijah, Elisha, David, Solomon, Isaiah, Daniel and Zechariah.

On the other hand, it is also amazing that Jesus never once quoted from the Old Testament book of the prophet Ezekiel. The book of Ezekiel contains nearly 40,000 words of flaming prophecy. Yet Jesus never quoted the book of Ezekiel. Not once. Jesus never even alluded to Ezekiel. Nor did he ever mention an historical fact known only from the book of Ezekiel. In short, from the statements of Jesus recorded in the New Testament a reader would never suspect the prophet Ezekiel ever

1

existed. Yet in the New Testament Jesus directly quoted the prophet Hosea, whose book contains a mere 5000 words — not once but twice!

Can today's Christian explain such amazing facts? And will the explanations increase understanding of Jesus and the Old Testament? The apostle Paul only deepens the mystery of preferences with his letters recorded in the New Testament. Like Jesus, Paul never quoted Ezekiel in the New Testament. Yet Paul quoted the prophet Habakkuk twice. The book of Habakkuk is a tiny Old Testament book, with little more than 1000 words. Can today's Christian explain the fact that Paul preferred such a tiny book to the huge book of Ezekiel? Like Jesus, Paul never alluded to Ezekiel either. Nor did he ever mention an historical fact known only from Ezekiel. In short, from Paul's letters recorded in the New Testament a reader would never suspect the prophet Ezekiel ever existed.

The astonishing omission of Ezekiel in the New Testament does not stop with the recorded testimony of Jesus and Paul. No quote of Ezekiel is in the New Testament from those who wrote the narratives of Matthew, Mark, Luke, John and Acts. No quote of Ezekiel is in the New Testament from Peter's letters. No quote of Ezekiel is in the New Testament from John's letters. No quote of Ezekiel is in the New Testament from the writer of the book of Hebrews. In fact, no quote of Ezekiel occurs anywhere in the New Testament. Nor is there an allusion to Ezekiel anywhere in the New Testament. Nor is any historical fact known only from Ezekiel mentioned anywhere in the New Testament. In short, from the entire record of the New Testament a reader would never suspect the prophet Ezekiel ever existed.

Habakkuk, Hosea and Ezekiel are not the only examples of Old Testament books being quoted or not being quoted by Jesus and the writers of the New Testament. Examples abound. Jesus and the writers of the New Testament do not quote Esther, Ecclesiastes, Lamentations, Song of Songs, Ezra or Nehemiah. In fact Jesus and the writers of the New Testament do not refer to those books in any way. Not once. The New Testament mentions Ruth only one time and never quotes her book at all. Did Jesus and the writers of the New Testament quote Judges, Joshua, Chronicles and Obadiah? No. And do they quote Jonah, Nahum and Zephaniah? No again. In fact, of the 39 books of the Old Testament, Jesus and the writers of the New Testament quoted only 21. Of those 21 books they quoted only 12 more than twice.

Yet there is a Bible that Jesus loved. There is a Bible that Paul loved. And there is a Bible the other followers of Jesus loved.

Can today's Christian determine that Bible in detail? Can today's Christian explain why Jesus and his followers loved certain books? Can today's Christian explain why Jesus and his followers shunned other books? And will the explanations increase understanding of Jesus, his followers and the Old Testament? Answering these questions is the very goal of this book: The Bible Jesus Loved. For this book investigates in detail the preferences and omissions of books in the Old Testament by Jesus and his followers.

This book owes a heavy debt to the diligent scholars who decipher quotes of the Old Testament in the New Testament. Roger Nicole defined the process well.

> [There are] 224 direct citations introduced by a definite formula indicating the writer purposed to quote. To these must be added 7 cases where a second quotation is introduced by the conjunction "and," and 19 cases where a paraphrase or summary rather than a direct quotation follows the introductory formula....[3]

Thus Nicole identified 250 quotes of the Old Testament in the New.

Scholars like Nicole usually identify about 250 to 300 quotes of the Old Testament in the New Testament. Appendix A of this book offers such a list based on three scholarly studies. Appendix A lists 247 quotations of the Old Testament in the New Testament, lessened in number by the removal of redundancies. There are reasonable grounds for the varying number of direct quotes of the Old Testament in the New Testament among scholars. These reasons are discussed in subsequent chapters. The number of direct quotations in real dispute however is a small amount of the total number.

The number of allusions to the Old Testament in the New Testament however is another matter. Allusions are much more numerous than direct quotations, and by their nature allusions are not as well defined. The number of allusions varies greatly from scholar to scholar. The study of allusions adds much less toward the objectives of this book than the study of direct quotes. In subsequent chapters broad allusions to Biblical figures may be mentioned but not quantified.

Now let us move on to study the Bible Jesus loved.

< 2 >

WHAT WAS THE BIBLE JESUS LOVED?

Of course Jesus did not call Holy Scriptures of the Jews the 'Old Testament'. Christians applied the 'Old Testament' name after they had established their 'New Testament'. First known use of 'New Testament' was by Christian theologian Tertullian in about 200 AD.[4] It seems logical that 'Old Testament' usage began about then too. But Jesus referred to the Holy Scriptures of the Jews several ways. He called them simply the 'Scriptures' as he did in Matthew 21:42 and several other passages. He also referred to them as 'the Law and the Prophets' as he did in Matthew 22:40 and several other verses. Once, in Luke 24:44, he uttered the nearly full-blown 'the Law of Moses, the Prophets and the Psalms'.

But what constituted Holy Scriptures of the Jews for Jesus? Note at the outset that this is not going to focus on which books properly belong in the present-day Old Testament of Christians. Bible students know that Catholics and Protestants disagree on the books known as the Apocrypha. Catholics include them; Protestants do not. No, the concern now is with what Jesus and his contemporary Jews considered Holy Scriptures. Also note at the outset that Holy Scriptures for Jesus were inked on long rolled scrolls, not in 'books' — although this distinction will not be noted again and again.

The esteemed Jewish historian Josephus, who lived from 37 to 101 AD, provided answers as to what 'books' the Jews considered Holy Scriptures. In his tract "Against Apion" Josephus declared of Jewish Scriptures, "Although such long ages have now gone by, no one has dared to add anything to them, to take away anything from them, or to change anything in them."[5] So in the day of Jesus and his followers the Jewish Scriptures were established and apparently rigid.

Many ancient sources attested to a three-fold division of Jewish Holy Scriptures. In "Against Apion" Josephus confirmed the 'three-fold' Holy Scriptures for the Jews and expanded on it. The oldest divi-

4

sion included the five 'books of Moses' in this order: Genesis, Exodus, Leviticus, Numbers and Deuteronomy. From earliest days the Jews also called the five books of Moses the 'Torah', a Hebrew word for 'Law' or 'teaching'. Unfortunately the meaning of 'Torah' evolved in later use often to include all the Jewish Scriptures. A Greek word for 'five books', the 'Pentateuch' (pronounced pent´-ah-tyuke), came into common use and remains more precise for Genesis, Exodus, Leviticus, Numbers and Deuteronomy.

The second division of Jewish Holy Scriptures included eight books of the 'Nebum', a Hebrew word for 'Prophets'. Prophets were designated 'Former' and 'Latter'. First came the four books of the former prophets in this order: Joshua, Judges, Samuel and Kings. Then in no rigid order came four books of the latter prophets: Isaiah, Jeremiah, Ezekiel and the 'Twelve'. The 'Twelve' were twelve prophets whose prophecies were all inscribed on one scroll: Hosea, Joel, Amos, Obadiah, Jonah, Micah, Nahum, Habakkuk, Zephaniah, Haggai, Zechariah and Malachi. To Christians the 'Twelve' traditionally referred to the twelve disciples of Jesus. But here and in all subsequent discussions the 'Twelve' refers to a specific group of twelve prophets in the Old Testament.

The third division of the Jewish Holy Scriptures was made up of the eleven books of the 'Kethubim', Hebrew for 'Writings'. In no particular order were ten books: Psalms, Proverbs, Job, Song of Songs, Ruth, Lamentations, Ecclesiastes, Esther, Daniel and Ezra-Nehemiah. It was however customary to end the 'Kethubim' — and in fact all Jewish Holy Scriptures — with the book of Chronicles. Note that neither Jesus nor his followers ever referred to the Kethubim as the 'Writings'. If they referred to this third division at all they called it simply 'the Psalms'. Note also that the 'Writings' include the prominent prophet Daniel.

In summary Jesus read Jewish Holy Scriptures that had three divisions including twenty-four 'books'. Often ancient Jews appended Ruth to Judges and Lamentations to Jeremiah. This yielded 22 books, one book for each letter of the Hebrew alphabet.[6] Even well-documented evidence from Josephus and others does not completely put the matter to rest. The reason for this is the presence of the Septuagint. This was a version of the Jewish Scriptures — not in Hebrew but in Greek. The Septuagint was the effort of scholarly Jews living in Egypt about 200 years before Jesus. They wanted to provide their Holy Scriptures in the common language of the vast area conquered by Alexander the Great. Because the Septuagint was in Greek, it did in fact become popular and widespread.

One problem the Septuagint introduced was that some of its manuscripts included books unknown in the Hebrew Holy Scriptures of the Jews. These were known eventually as the books of Wisdom, Judith, Tobit, Ecclesiasticus and the Macabees. The Catholic Church incorporated them into its Old Testament. The Protestants recognize them collectively as the 'Apocrypha' but exclude them from their Old Testament. There is no evidence Jesus and his followers considered them Holy Scriptures. They never once quoted or alluded to any of the books of the Apocrypha.[7]

Note that Jesus did not regard as holy the Jewish oral law — the 'tradition of the elders' — touted by some Jewish sects.[8] Jesus believed many of the oral laws were created to skirt the Jewish Holy Scriptures. He confirmed this by his outburst in Mark 7:6–9:

> Isaiah was right when he prophesied about you hypocrites; as it is written:
> 'These people honor me with their lips, but their hearts are far from me.
> They worship me in vain; their teachings are but rules taught by men.'

Jesus had quoted Isaiah 29:13 in Mark, then added:

> You have let go of the commands of God and are holding on to the traditions of men. You have a fine way of setting aside the commands of God in order to observe your own traditions!

Although Jesus and his followers probably did not recognize as holy the Apocryphal books in the Septuagint, they did often quote the Septuagint. In addition, in their native language of Aramaic they also often paraphrased their Hebrew version of Holy Scriptures. This paraphrased Scripture in Aramaic was called a 'Targum'. Possible versions do not even end there. The Dead Sea Scrolls, discovered in 1947, are Hebrew texts much older than the 'Masoretic' text, which was long considered the standard Hebrew text. The Dead Sea scrolls actually date before the time of Jesus. In some cases these scrolls have authenticated quotations of Old Testament passages in the New Testament that previously were considered inaccurate.

And yet, Jesus and his followers may have quoted yet another version of Holy Scriptures. Scholars think they may have occasionally quoted the Pentateuch of the Samaritans, which preserved a Hebrew text that may also be older than the Masoretic text. Thus, at least five sources of quotes from the Old Testament are possible: Septuagint, Masoretic Hebrew, 'Targum', Dead Sea Hebrew and the Samaritan Pentateuch! Subsequent chapters in this book however will not attempt to quantify these various Old Testament sources quoted by Jesus and his followers in the New Testament.[9]

Why were Jesus and his followers seemingly so flexible about which version they quoted? It is likely they exercised flexibility to suit their particular audience. Their listeners or readers may have been Jews who best understood Hebrew and/or Aramaic. Or their listeners or readers may have been Jews or Gentiles who best understood Greek. Later narratives written for books of the New Testament also aimed at specific groups. For example, scholars think the book of Matthew targeted Jews with proofs that Jesus was the long awaited Messiah. On the other hand, the writer of the books of Luke and Acts may have written for the Gentiles. These comments however about selection of source for intended audience are generalities. Exceptions are many. For example, the book of Matthew (Matthew 1:23), supposedly aimed at Jews, quoted the Septuagint version of Isaiah 7:14, 'The virgin will be with child and will give birth to a son'. Why? Some scholars believe Matthew quoted the Septuagint because the Greek 'parthenos' meant specifically a virgin whereas the less specific Hebrew 'almah' meant a young unmarried woman.

To record a quote in the Greek of the New Testament, the writer had to retranslate the quote if it was originally in Aramaic or Hebrew. This suggests an additional complication for identifying the scriptural source. Moreover, scholar John Wenham pointed out that a New Testament writer may well have adapted a different syntax for a quotation in order to integrate the quotation smoothly into his own writing style.[10] Can this be proven? Not with certainty. Naturally the New Testament writer did not specify what he was doing in that respect. This kind of modification also explains why it may be difficult sometimes to determine if a New Testament passage is even a direct quotation of an Old Testament book.

What can today's Christian conclude about the Jewish Holy Scriptures that Jesus and his followers knew? First, it is entirely plausible that 'the Law, the Prophets and the Psalms' spoken of by Jesus as Jewish Holy Scriptures were what is now the Old Testament of Protestants (in subsequent chapters 'Holy Scriptures' or 'Jewish Scriptures' will be used interchangeably with 'Old Testament'). Second, Jesus and his followers were very flexible about which version of the Holy Scriptures they quoted.[11]

But move on to the actual books they favored.

For there is clearly a Bible Jesus Loved!

< 3 >

'BOOKS' OF THE BIBLE JESUS AND HIS FOLLOWERS QUOTED

Now the discussion shifts to the focus of this study: which books of Jewish Holy Scriptures did Jesus and his followers love so much they quoted from them? For there is clearly a Bible Jesus Loved. One distinguished Bible scholar, W. D. Davies, insisted that the quotations from the Old Testament in the New Testament are profoundly significant.[12] Tapping into that profound significance is the goal of this book. The first step is the actual compilation of direct quotations of the Old Testament in various books of the New Testament. The method of counting occurrences of quotations will be explained first.

The three synoptic Gospels — Matthew, Mark and Luke — present a unique problem. It is widely accepted by scholars that Matthew and Luke incorporated Mark into their own Gospels. Of Mark's 661 verses, over 600 of them were duplicated in Matthew and 350 of them were duplicated in Luke. Mark had only 31 verses not found in the other two. For the purposes of tabulating Old Testament quotations in these three Gospels it is obvious the same quotation should not be tallied three times. Therefore in the compilation of Appendix A such a quote is shown only once — and it is attributed to Mark.

Similarly, scholars have long believed Matthew and Luke also incorporated an unknown source (called 'Q' by a German scholar).[13] The compilation likewise avoids this duplication, with precedence arbitrarily given to Luke. Another cause of duplication in a study of this kind is the Old Testament source itself being replicated. In this study if a passage quoted in the New Testament was found more than once in the Old Testament, the passage is attributed to its first occurrence in Jewish Holy Scriptures (that is, according to their order as we know it today). This repetition was especially common between Exodus and Deuteronomy. Such a passage is attributed to Exodus.[14]

In addition to the above process of counting occurrences, this study distinguished three categories of New Testament 'lovers' of the

Jewish Holy Scriptures. First lover of course is Jesus. Jesus spoke to us from the four Gospels (Matthew, Mark, Luke and John), Acts and Revelations. The second category of lover is Paul, evidenced by all the letters written by Paul, as well as Paul's spoken words in Acts.[15] The third category of lover includes the narrative portions of the four Gospels, Acts and Revelations — that is, the text where Jesus (or Paul) is not speaking. This third category also includes all the New Testament letter writers other than Paul. In all subsequent discussions, this third category is dubbed the 'Other New Testament Writers' or also frequently the 'followers of Jesus' (other than Paul).

JESUS

Within the ground rules above, consider which books of Jewish Holy Scriptures (or Christian Old Testament) Jesus loved. In the four Gospels, Acts and the book of Revelations he quotes the Old Testament 41 times:

BOOK	QUOTATIONS	
Genesis	2	
Exodus	7	
Leviticus	2	
Deuteronomy	6	
Total from the Pentateuch ('Law')		17
Psalms	10	
Daniel	1	
Total from the Writings		11
Isaiah	8	
Jeremiah	1	
Hosea	2	
Micah	1	
Zechariah	1	
Total from the Prophets		13

Clearly Jesus emphasized the Pentateuch or 'Law'. However all three divisions of Jewish Scriptures — the 'Law', the 'Writings' and the 'Prophets' — are well represented. But within the three divisions lurk imbalances. His preference among the Writings was almost solely from the Psalms. His only other quote from the Writings was Daniel.[16] He never quoted Job or Proverbs. Among the Prophets he clearly favored Isaiah. Of the many prophets, other than Jeremiah he favored those from the 'Twelve'. The Pentateuch, the Psalms, the book of

Isaiah and the 'Twelve' account for **95 percent** of his direct quotes of Holy Scriptures. The unmistakable conclusion is that Jesus most loved the Pentateuch, the Psalms, the book of Isaiah and the 'Twelve'.

What of his broad allusions? Jesus spoke often of Old Testament figures. He noted Abraham nine times. He spoke of Moses 13 times and David eight times. He also remarked on Abel, Daniel, Elijah, Elisha, Isaac, Jacob, Jezebel, Jonah, Lot, Noah, Queen of the South, Solomon and Zechariah. In this way he further revealed his knowledge of the Pentateuch and the historical books the Jews included in the 'Prophets'. Furthermore, scholar John Wenham asserts Jesus considered the stories told by these books not symbolic but factual.[17]

PAUL

Now consider the preferences among the 108 quotations of the Old Testament by Paul in Acts and in his many letters[18]:

BOOK	QUOTATIONS	
Genesis	14	
Exodus	10	
Leviticus	5	
Numbers	1	
Deuteronomy	10	
Total from the Pentateuch ('Law')		40
Job	2	
Psalms	22	
Proverbs	1	
Total from the Writings		25
2 Samuel	2	
1 Kings	2	
Isaiah	28	
Jeremiah	3	
Hosea	3	
Joel	1	
Habakkuk	3	
Malachi	1	
Total from the Prophets		43

What emerges for the quotations by Paul is almost the same balance among the Pentateuch, the Writings and the Prophets found in the quotations of Jesus. Paul slightly favored the Prophets over the Pentateuch. He least favored the Writings. However, once again marked imbalances occur within the divisions. Paul preferred Psalms almost exclusively to the other Writings. Paul quoted eight prophets, of which he strongly favored Isaiah but also esteemed the Twelve. The Pentateuch, the Psalms, the book of Isaiah and the Twelve account for **91 percent** of Paul's direct quotes of Holy Scriptures. The unmistakable conclusion is that Paul loved the Pentateuch, the Psalms, the book of Isaiah and the Twelve.

What of Paul's broad allusions? He too spoke of Old Testament figures. He mentioned Abraham, Moses and David. He also remarked on Adam, Elijah, Eve, Isaac, Jacob and Jesse. Paul certainly revealed knowledge of the Pentateuch and the historical books the Jews included in the 'Prophets'. He also accepted the stories told by these books as historical facts, not symbols.

OTHER FOLLOWERS OF JESUS

Direct quotations of the Old Testament by the Other New Testament writers (or followers of Jesus other than Paul) number 98. Specifically these include with the exception of Paul all the other New Testament letter writers (Hebrews, James, 1 Peter, 2 Peter, 1 John, 2 John, 3 John, Jude and Revelation) and also the writers of the narratives of Matthew, Mark, Luke, John and Acts. Did the preferences of followers of Jesus other than Paul differ from those of Jesus? Or of Paul's?

Here is a summary:

BOOK	QUOTATIONS	
Genesis	8	
Exodus	10	
Leviticus	3	
Deuteronomy	6	
Total from Pentateuch ('Law')		27
Psalms	28	
Proverbs	6	
Daniel	1	
Total from the Writings		35

2 Samuel	1
Isaiah	20
Jeremiah	2
Hosea	2
Joel	1
Amos	2
Micah	1
Habakkuk	1
Haggai	1
Zechariah	4
Malachi	1
Total from the Prophets	36

Once again the three divisions of Jewish Scriptures — the Law, the Writings and the Prophets — were each adequately represented. But the followers of Jesus other than Paul favored the Prophets and the Writings more than the Pentateuch. This group of New Testament writers, more than Jesus and Paul, emphasized the Writings. Again within the divisions lurk imbalances. Although the other New Testament writers often quoted Proverbs among the Writings, they much preferred Psalms. Although they quoted 11 prophets, they much preferred Isaiah but also esteemed the Twelve. As a result, the Pentateuch, the Psalms, the book of Isaiah and the Twelve account for **90 percent** of their direct quotes of Holy Scriptures. The unmistakable conclusion is that the other New Testament writers (or followers of Jesus other than Paul) loved the Pentateuch, the Psalms, the book of Isaiah and the Twelve.

What of their broad allusions? The New Testament writers other than Paul wrote often of Old Testament figures. Frequently they remarked on Abraham, Moses and David. They also mentioned Aaron, Abel, Adam, Balaam, Barak, Cain, Elijah, Enoch, Gideon, Isaac, Jacob, Jephthah, Jesse, Job, Joseph, Joshua, Korah, Lot, Melchizedek, Noah, Rahab, Samuel, Samson, Saul and Solomon. These references of course revealed knowledge of the Pentateuch and the historical books the Jews included in the 'Prophets'. The New Testament writers also accepted the stories told by these books as factual, not symbolic.

JESUS AND ALL HIS FOLLOWERS

Now look at the totals for Jesus and all his followers as recorded in the New Testament:

BOOK	QUOTATIONS	
Genesis	24	
Exodus	27	
Leviticus	10	
Numbers	1	
Deuteronomy	22	
Total from Pentateuch ('Law')		84
Job	2	
Psalms	60	
Proverbs	7	
Daniel	2	
Total from the Writings		71
2 Samuel	3	
1 Kings	2	
Isaiah	56	
Jeremiah	6	
Hosea	7	
Joel	2	
Amos	2	
Micah	2	
Habakkuk	4	
Haggai	1	
Zechariah	5	
Malachi	2	
Total from the Prophets		92

In summary Jesus and all his followers quoted the Pentateuch extensively — 84 times in all. They all effusively quoted the Writings, but their overwhelming source among the 71 quotes from the Writings was the book of Psalms. They all liberally quoted the Prophets, but clearly the chief source for the 92 quotes was the book of Isaiah but also the Twelve.

Overall, the Pentateuch, the book of Psalms, the book of Isaiah and the Twelve account for 225 of the 247 quotations of the Old Testament in the New Testament by Jesus and all his followers — or a convincing 91 percent![19]

Can there be any doubt that these books — the Pentateuch, the Psalms, Isaiah and the Twelve — were the heart of the Bible Jesus loved? Also, can there be any doubt that these books — the Pentateuch, Psalms, Isaiah and the Twelve — were the heart of the Bible the followers of Jesus loved?

Subsequent chapters examine each of these four principal sources of inspiration — the Pentateuch, the Psalms, Isaiah and the Twelve — for Jesus and his followers.

Begin with the Pentateuch...

< 4 >

MESSAGE OF THE 'LAW' (THE PENTATEUCH)

Quotations from the 'Law' — or the Pentateuch — number 84 in the New Testament. That is slightly more than one-third of the total of 247 quotations by Jesus and his followers. Why did Jesus and his followers so love the Pentateuch? What was the message from the Pentateuch? As noted before, the Pentateuch was the Greek name for the first five books of the Jewish Holy Scriptures (which are as well the first five books of the Christian Old Testament). The Pentateuch constituted about one-fourth of the Jewish Scriptures. It was the core of Judaism. All sects of Judaism accepted the five books of the Pentateuch as sacred. It was sacred even to the often-disparaged Samaritans.

Tradition attributed the authorship of all five books to Moses. However, liberal scholarship of the last 250 years has theorized the compilation and blending of several different documents. The French physician Jean Astruc began the assault in the 1700's. He speculated that calling God both 'Elohim' and 'Yahweh' in Genesis meant two different sources. By the mid-20th Century liberal scholars 'recognized' seven different documents in Genesis alone. They spawned so many theories about the Pentateuch that today there is no consensus among them. Liberal scholars continue to dissect these sacred writings. They dismiss the assertion of Philo, a distinguished Jewish historian in the first century AD, that the Jews "have not altered a single word of what had been written by him" — meaning the five books of Moses.[20]

To understand the Pentateuch it must be considered as a whole, regardless of authorship. The Pentateuch has unifying themes. Scholar Derek Kidner pointed out that beginning with Genesis the Old Testament has a forward thrust toward events that it prophesied.[21] At its greatest relevance to Christians, the Pentateuch foreshadowed Jesus the Messiah. At its least, the Pentateuch may have done no less than lay the foundation of western civilization. Secular scholars invariably credit western civilization to only Greeks and Romans. A plausible case can be made that western civilization grew out of much older Jewish roots.

Genesis, the first book of the Pentateuch, is a cosmic epic that spans creation to the end of the first four generations of the Jewish patriarchs. The debate between an 'old earth' and a 'young earth' is beyond the scope of this book. The best treatment of very few 'young earth' scenarios is by the Jewish physicist Gerald Schroeder.[22] Be content to know that the first patriarch Abraham was born about 2200 years before Jesus was born. Joseph — of the fourth generation — died in about 1800 BC. Exodus, the next book of the Pentateuch, sped forward 300 years to the birth of Moses. The Pentateuch ended about 1400 BC — with the death of Moses.

But why let concerns over time distract from the cosmic magnificence of Genesis? With mind-expanding rapidity the reader of Genesis encounters creation, paradise, the advent of mankind in Adam and Eve, Satanic influence, the concept of good and evil, mankind's failure to be faithful, mankind's death, and eventually God's destruction of the unfaithful with a vast flood. Mankind had violated the 'covenant' God made with them. Through the faithful Noah God gave mankind a second chance. With Abraham, who proved his faithfulness, God made the first 'covenant' that endured. In Genesis 12:1–2 God said to Abraham:

> Leave your country, your people and your father's
>   household and go to the land I will show you.
> I will make you into a great nation and I will bless
>   you...

Thus, God made three promises. One promise was that Abraham's line — the Jews — would become a great nation. A second was that God would bless the Jews. The third promise was that the Jews would receive land. These promises were kept by God, but the process took hundreds of years. In fact by the end of the eight centuries of the Pentateuch the Jews were only on the brink of claiming their promised land.

In Genesis, the line of Abraham — extended through Isaac, then Jacob and finally Joseph — survived threat after threat. Joseph prospered in Egypt, but his descendants did not. Eventually all the Jews were enslaved in Egypt. Exodus, second book of the Pentateuch, relates how Moses led the Jews out of slavery hundreds of years after Joseph. Moreover, God then selected Moses to deliver to the Jews the

Ten Commandments and other laws. Leviticus, the third book of the Pentateuch, adds many other commandments of the 'law' to the covenant. The book of Numbers narrates the 38 years of wandering by Moses and the Jews in the desert—from Mount Sinai to the plains of Moab on the border of Canaan. Because the Jews were disobedient at times, those from Egypt—even Moses himself—never entered the Promised Land. Only their children survived to enter Canaan. Deuteronomy, final book of the Pentateuch, was a book that repeated the laws. Yet it was a loving book, virtually the 'swan song' of Moses. Thus the books of Exodus, Leviticus, Numbers and Deuteronomy— bound together by the narrative of Moses' life—end with his death.

Don't assume the five books were called the 'Law' only because of the Ten Commandments. The Pentateuch contains over 600 laws! Some seem quaint today—even laughable—like "Do not cook a young goat in its mother's milk", a law found no less than three times in the Pentateuch.[23] Why would God give the Jews a law that seems to us so silly? The answer was once reasonable. At that time in the history of the Jews, neighboring pagans practiced this custom of cooking a young goat in its mother's milk. It was a barbaric superstition to promote fertility. Be mindful also that outside the Pentateuch with its over 600 laws there are virtually no other laws in the entire Old Testament! So is it any wonder Jews called the Pentateuch the 'Law'?

Was the Jewish 'Law' any different from the laws of Hammurabi and other codes of law in antiquity? Yes. First of all, Jewish law claimed God as its authority. Other codes of law claimed the reigning king as authority. One code was God-given, the others were secular. Moreover, Jewish law was applied universally. Other law codes of antiquity were applied differently to different social levels—with special preference given to the aristocracy. So God-given Jewish 'Law' was far more profound and equitable than other codes of laws in antiquity. Do not be misled into thinking the Jews were just like any other 'culture' in antiquity.

Besides documenting the Jews as the chosen people and giving them laws to live by, the Pentateuch introduced three theological concepts that were far more profound than any of the surrounding pagan religions. First, consider the nature of God. A team of scholars noted the Mesopotamians—from whom Abraham arose—were hostile to 'monotheism' or 'one God', and added that the same could be said for other peoples of antiquity.[24] Yes, the Jews worshipped a purposeful

Creator while the Greeks and Romans were worshipping armadas of whimsical gods and goddesses. Only Jews worshipped one God.[25] The God of the Pentateuch was a living God, a purposeful God involved in history. He was not aloof. His ways were mysterious to mankind but perfect. He chose to reveal himself, first to Adam, then to Noah, then to the Jewish patriarchs. He was not monolithic. He appeared in many forms: in dreams, in a burning bush, as a man or as an angel.

Second, consider the nature of mankind. The Pentateuch showed mankind was not 'basically good' — but basically flawed. This flawed nature resulted from the same paradox — God's gift of free will — that caused some angels to sin. Mankind also fell. The sin of Adam and Eve in paradise resulted not only in death but a life of hard toil. Still, it was with these very flawed men and women that God made more covenants. It was flawed mankind that God wanted to save.

Salvation was the third profound theological concept. In the Pentateuch salvation also involved grace and election. God's elections were revealed repeatedly. He 'elected' Abraham and Sarah, both old and childless, to launch the Jewish nation. He elected Isaac over Ishmael, and Jacob over Esau. Yet salvation in the Pentateuch contained only the slightest hint of a believer's survival after physical death. God's edict of Genesis 3:19, "for dust you are and to dust you will return" was gloomy indeed. Even though Genesis 5:24 implied Enoch did not die but "God took him away", the Jews in the time of Moses probably did not entertain any hope of life after death.[26] So, although the concepts of God, man and salvation in the Pentateuch were profound they only foreshadowed the good news of the New Testament.

Prophecies of the Messiah in the Pentateuch were few, compared to the later parts of the Jewish Holy Scriptures. Scholar John Walvoord found about 100 Messianic prophesies in the entire Old Testament.[27] Of that total only 15 occur in the Pentateuch. Walvoord attributed 10 to Genesis, one to Exodus, two to Numbers and two to Deuteronomy. Some prophecies Walvoord deemed Messianic are very subtle. Some are vague, seeming to prophesy the nation of Israel or future prophets rather than a Messiah. But on the other hand a few are very suggestive of the Messiah. These will be discussed in coming chapters.

Now, consider just how Jesus and his followers loved the five books of Moses...

< 5 >

HOW JESUS LOVED THE 'LAW'

Jesus quoted the 'Law' — or the Pentateuch — 17 times!

He clearly attributed authorship of the Pentateuch to Moses. Some scholars argue that Jesus never meant to include Genesis in the 'books of Moses', but this is a distinction never made by Jesus and his followers. Two examples of Jesus speaking of Moses — John 5:45-46 and Luke 24:25-27 — would be much weakened if Genesis were excluded from the 'books of Moses'. Luke 24:44 also illustrates this point, when Jesus said:

> This is what I told you while I was still with you: Everything must be fulfilled that is written about me in the Law of Moses, the Prophets and the Psalms.

It is unreasonable to think that Jesus did not also refer to the Messianic prophecy from God contained in Genesis 49:10:

> The scepter will not depart from Judah, nor the ruler's staff from between his feet, until he comes to whom it belongs and the obedience of the nations is his.

Most of the direct quotes of the Pentateuch by Jesus — in fact, 10 of them — were in response to hostile questions. Before Jesus began his ministry (and confrontations with Jewish authorities) he had to contend with the most hostile antagonist on earth: Satan! Three times in Luke 4:3-12 Jesus quoted the book of Deuteronomy (8:3, 6:13, 6:16) to refute Satan's temptations in the wilderness.

> The devil said to him, "If you are the Son of God, tell this stone to become bread."
> Jesus answered, "It is written: 'Man does not live on bread alone.'"
> The devil led him up to a high place and showed him in an instant all the kingdoms of the world. And he said to him, "I will give you all their authority and splendor, for it has been

given to me, and I can give it to anyone I want to. So if you worship me, it will all be yours."

Jesus answered, "It is written: 'Worship the Lord your God and serve him only.'"

The devil led him to Jerusalem and had him stand on the highest point of the temple. "If you are the Son of God," he said, "throw yourself down from here. For it is written:

'He will command his angels concerning you
to guard you carefully; they will lift you up in their hands,
so that you will not strike your foot against a stone.'"

Jesus answered, "It says: 'Do not put the Lord your God to the test.'"

Then the devil left him. Note that Psalms 91:11–12 was quoted by the devil! But Jesus made use of Deuteronomy, which emphasized God's covenant with the Jews. That covenant demanded absolute allegiance to God.

Seven direct quotes of the Pentateuch were responses by Jesus to hostile questions from the 'chief priests, the teachers of the law and the elders'. Holy Scriptures were irrefutable to them too. Many times — often at the Temple — he quoted the Pentateuch to Jewish authorities in answer to a question with which they hoped to elicit either a heresy or a political gaffe.

On one occasion his antagonists hoped Jesus would answer a question about divorce in such a way as to anger Herod Antipas (just as John the Baptist had angered him). Herod was 'married' to the wife of his own still-living brother. Jesus answered his antagonists that Moses had indeed permitted divorce. But then Jesus combined quotes from Genesis 1:27 and 2:24 to add:

But at the beginning of creation God 'made them male and female.' 'For this reason a man will leave his father and mother and be united to his wife, and the two will become one flesh.' So they are no longer two, but one. Therefore what God has joined together, let man not separate. (Mark 10:6–9)

Jesus made the point that Moses had made divorce easier for the Jews but that leniency was not in harmony with God's intentions. Did this answer anger Herod? Undoubtedly.

In his Sermon on the Mount — recorded in chapters 5 and 6 of Matthew — Jesus had been even more specific, applying the words of Moses in Deuteronomy 24:1 (Matthew 5:31–32):

It has been said, 'Anyone who divorces his wife must give her a certificate of divorce.' But I tell you that anyone who divorces his wife, except for marital unfaithfulness, causes her to become an adulteress, and anyone who marries the divorced woman commits adultery.

This was not an assertion that the law in the Holy Scriptures was invalid. It was an integral part of his Sermon on the Mount message: in love try to attain perfection. Yes, perhaps divorce was permitted, but it fell short of God's desire for men and women.

On another occasion Jesus and his disciples were accused of not observing the 'law'. In answer Jesus combined two quotes from the Pentateuch, Exodus 20:12 and 21:17:

You have a fine way of setting aside the commands of God in order to observe your own traditions! For Moses said, 'Honor your father and your mother,' and, 'Anyone who curses his father or mother must be put to death.' But you say that if a man says to his father or mother: 'Whatever help you might otherwise have received from me is Corban' (that is, a gift devoted to God), then you no longer let him do anything for his father or mother. Thus you nullify the word of God by your tradition that you have handed down. And you do many things like that. (Mark 7:9–13)

In this case Jesus pointed out how oral laws established by tradition contradicted the laws of the Pentateuch. The concept of 'Corban' was cynical in that it justified a son's neglect of his parents on the grounds he was giving the money to God. In fact the money was going to the priests in the Temple.

Another time Jesus was challenged by Sadducees, a powerful Jewish sect that did not believe in resurrection. In Mark 12:26 Jesus answered them by quoting God in Exodus 3:6, "I am the God of Abraham, the God of Isaac and the God of Jacob". In other words, would God say 'I am' if Abraham, Isaac and Jacob were truly lost to the grave forever?

On another occasion while at the Temple debating 'the chief priests, the teachers of the law and the elders', Jesus combined two passages, the first passage from Deuteronomy 6:4–5 and then the other one from Leviticus 19:18, to fuse all the laws into the two greatest commandments:

"The most important one," answered Jesus, "is this: 'Hear, O Israel, the Lord our God, the Lord is one. Love the Lord your God with all your heart and with all your soul and with all your mind and with all your strength.' The second is this: 'Love your neighbor as yourself.' There is no commandment greater than these." (Mark 12:29–31)[28]

Did Jesus love the Pentateuch — Moses' five books of Law — as Holy Scriptures? Most assuredly. The first commandment he quoted above was called the 'Shema' after the first Hebrew word for 'Hear' in the passage from Deuteronomy. It was virtually the Jewish confession of faith, recited by devout Jews morning and evening. Even today the 'Shema' begins every worship service in the synagogue.

The preceding 10 quotes of the authority of the Pentateuch were used by Jesus to fend off hostile questions. But Jesus made use of the Pentateuch in friendlier exchanges. To a rich young man who wanted confirmation that his good works would earn him eternal life, Jesus said in Mark 10:19:

You know the commandments: 'Do not murder, do not commit adultery, do not steal, do not give false testimony, do not defraud, honor your father and mother.'

The young man beamed. He had obeyed all these commandments in Exodus 20:12–16. Surely he had earned eternal life. But as Mark 10:21 recorded, Jesus was not through speaking:

"One thing you lack," he said. "Go, sell everything you have and give to the poor, and you will have treasure in heaven. Then come, follow me."

The young man left, broken-hearted, because he was very rich. He had learned how the message of love that Jesus carried went beyond the laws of the Holy Scriptures.

In his Sermon on the Mount Jesus repeatedly quoted Exodus, or its equivalent in Deuteronomy, to refresh for his listeners some of the Ten Commandments and how his listeners must obey them in love. In other words, just as required of the rich young man, the listener must go beyond literal obedience to the commandments. In Matthew 5:21–22 Jesus started with Exodus 20:13, then went well beyond it:

You have heard that it was said to the people long ago, 'Do not murder, and anyone who murders will be subject to judgment.'

> But I tell you that anyone who is angry with his brother will be subject to judgment...

Once alone with his disciples Jesus expanded on resolving angry disputes. Settle it privately he urged. But if that didn't work, then invoke Deuteronomy 19:15 for settling disputes: 'every matter may be established by the testimony of two or three witnesses' (Matthew 18:16).

In Matthew 5:27–28, also in the Sermon on the Mount, Jesus began with Exodus 20:14 — then he added more to it:

> You have heard that it was said, 'Do not commit adultery.' But I tell you that anyone who looks at a woman lustfully has already committed adultery with her in his heart.

Continuing the Sermon on the Mount in Matthew 5:33–37 Jesus reworded Leviticus 19:12, then added a warning:

> Again, you have heard that it was said to the people long ago, 'Do not break your oath, but keep the oaths you have made to the Lord.' But I tell you, Do not swear at all: either by heaven, for it is God's throne; or by the earth, for it is his footstool; or by Jerusalem, for it is the city of the Great King. And do not swear by your head, for you cannot make even one hair white or black. Simply let your 'Yes' be 'Yes,' and your 'No,' 'No'; anything beyond this comes from the evil one.

In Matthew 5:38–39, yet another Sermon on the Mount example, Jesus quoted Exodus 21:24, then added a restriction so 'hard' for the proud to understand:

> You have heard that it was said, 'Eye for eye, and tooth for tooth.' But I tell you, Do not resist an evil person. If someone strikes you on the right cheek, turn to him the other also.

In summary Jesus quoted the Pentateuch 17 times. He used it enlist authority, for he believed in it and those who contended with him also believed in it. He used it to foil hostile questions and he used it to instruct his followers. But he also frequently emphasized that slavish, loveless adherence to the laws of the Pentateuch was not enough. Nevertheless, Jesus clearly loved the Pentateuch.

Did the followers of Jesus like Paul love the Pentateuch?

< 6 >

HOW PAUL LOVED THE 'LAW'

Paul quoted the Pentateuch 40 times in the New Testament. Some may think this surprising. After all, didn't Paul denounce the 'Law'? No, Paul's attitude was in the same spirit as that of Jesus and his other followers. Careful reading reveals that Paul believed keeping the law in itself will not bring salvation but sin and death. To please God, one had to obey the 'Law' in love. The greatest commandment is to love. Without love the Law is nothing. Paul expressed this perfectly in 1 Corinthians 13. So when Paul appeared to ranting against the Law, in fact he was ranting against the use of the Law without love.[29]

Paul quoted the Pentateuch in many situations. In Acts 14:15 Luke recorded how Paul reacted when the crowd at Lystra declared he and Barnabas were gods:

> Men, why are you doing this? We too are only men, human like you. We are bringing you good news, telling you to turn from these worthless things to the living God, who made heaven and earth and sea and everything in them.

The phrase 'God, who made heaven and earth and sea and everything in them' was a quote from Exodus 20:11.

In Acts 23 Luke recorded the occasion when Paul was brought before the Sanhedrin. To defend himself against the charge that he insulted the high priest, Ananias, Paul claimed he did not know he was in front of the high priest and enlisted Exodus 22:28, "Do not speak evil about the ruler of your people." (Acts 23:5) Bible readers are often surprised by Paul's many staunch defenses of civil authorities. But that defense was an attitude right out of the Pentateuch.

Paul's book to the Romans was not so much a letter as it was a systematic discourse on theology. Bible scholar John Wenham summarized the book of Romans by noting that on the basis of Old Testament teaching Paul argued the extent and source of sin, justification by faith,

25

election, and the validity of the Gentile mission. Wenham pointed out that Paul established crucial points in the argument by extended scriptural quotations of the Old Testament.[30] Paul quoted the Pentateuch *16 times* in the book of Romans.

One great theme of Romans was that justification is by faith alone. Paul launched this argument in Romans 4:3 with Genesis 15:6: "Abraham believed God, and it was credited to him as righteousness." Paul went on to point out that Abraham — because of his faith — was the father of them all, employing in Romans 4:17 God's words in Genesis 17:5, "I have made you the father of many nations." And in Romans 4:18 Paul added God's words in Genesis 15:5, "And so shall your offspring be."

On another theme, in Romans 7:7 Paul used one of the Ten Commandments — "Do not covet" from Exodus 20:17 — as an example of the law. Here he developed a paradox: the knowledge of what is sinful produced a desire to sin and because of that sin, death. Was the law not good then? Paul insisted he delighted in God's law (Romans 7:22). This paradox is difficult to understand. Yet Genesis told the equivalent theme. Eating from the tree of the knowledge of good and evil caused the original sin and because of that sin, death!

In chapter 9 of Romans, with 'great sorrow and unceasing anguish' Paul argued yet another theme. To illustrate God's sovereign right to show mercy as he saw fit Paul quoted Genesis 21:12 and 18:14 for an example of electing Isaac over Ishmael and Genesis 25:23 for an example of electing Jacob over Esau. For more proof Paul made use of God's declaration to Moses in Exodus 33:19 (in Romans 9:15):

> I will have mercy on whom I have mercy, and I will have compassion on whom I have compassion.

In Romans 9:16 Paul cited as further proof of God's sovereign right Exodus 9:16, in which God declared to the Egyptian pharaoh:

> I raised you up for this very purpose, that I might display my power in you and that my name might be proclaimed in all the earth.

In verses 5 through 8 of Romans 10 Paul expanded his theme on 'God's rejection of Israel' and the failure of the 'Law'. First Paul quoted Moses' admonition to live by the Law in Leviticus 18:5, "The man who does these things will live by them", then Paul extracted the several phrases (indicated in italics) from Deuteronomy 30:12–14:

26

> It is not up in heaven, so that you have to ask, *"Who will ascend into heaven* to get it and proclaim it to us so we may obey it? Nor is it beyond the sea, so that you have to ask, *"Who will cross the sea* to get it and proclaim it to us so we may obey it? No, *the word is very near you; it is in your mouth and in your heart* so you may obey it.

The phrase 'Who will cross the sea' Paul quoted as 'Who will descend into the deep', indicating a source other than the Masoretic Hebrew text. Paul used the passage by Moses to show not that the 'Law' was very near but that Christ was very near. In verse 9 Paul continued:

> ...if you confess with your mouth, "Jesus is Lord", and believe in your heart that God raised him from the dead, you will be saved.

This of course is a well-known, often-quoted formula for salvation.

Paul lamented Israel's 'rejection' of Christ. Paul equated that to God's anger with the backsliding of the Jews in Deuteronomy 32:21 (quoted in Romans 10:19):

> I will make you envious by those who are not a nation; I will make you angry by a nation that has no understanding.

In Chapter 12 of Romans, on practicing righteousness Paul discouraged repaying anyone evil for evil, then used (in Romans 12:21) God's edict in Deuteronomy 32:35 for authority: 'It is mine to avenge; I will repay.' This was yet another example of how Jesus and his followers accepted the 'Law' as defining good and evil, but knew keeping the 'Law' alone did not bring salvation.

In Romans 13:9 Paul equated five of the Ten Commandments found in Exodus 20:13–15 to the one great commandment of Leviticus 19:18: "Love your neighbor as yourself." Then in Romans 13:10 he concluded, "Therefore, love is the fulfillment of the law." In Romans 15:10 Paul comforted the Romans with this quote from Deuteronomy 32:43: "Rejoice, O Gentiles, with his people."

The next great uses of quotations of the Pentateuch were in Paul's two letters to the Corinthians, each with five quotations — ten in all. His letters to the Corinthians were not expositions of theology. They addressed specific problems within the young church at Corinth in Greece. In 1 Corinthians 5:13 for obvious reasons he bluntly cited "Expel the wicked man among you", a demand that was found in Deuteronomy five times, the first time in Deuteronomy 17:7. In 1 Corinthians

6:15 Paul asked, "Do you not know that your bodies are members of Christ himself?" Then in the next verse (6:16) he quoted Genesis 2:24, "The two will become one flesh", in horror that a man would unite his body — part of Christ himself — with a prostitute. In 1 Corinthians 9:9 he defended his rights to food and drink while working as an apostle by applying a law in Deuteronomy 25:04: "Do not muzzle an ox while it is treading out the grain." In 1 Corinthians 10:7 he warned the young church not to sin as most of Moses' followers did in the desert (Exodus 32:6): "The people sat down to eat and drink and got up to indulge in pagan revelry." In 1 Corinthians 15:45 Paul used Genesis 2:7, "The first man Adam became a living being", to contrast with Christ, "the last Adam, a life-giving spirit."

In Paul's second letter to the Corinthians he quoted the Pentateuch another five times. It is obvious Paul accepted the truth of the Old Testament. The quotations seemingly came to him effortlessly. In speaking of how bold his hope was in the new covenant he made use of Exodus 34:33 in 2 Corinthians 3:13, "We are not like Moses, who would put a veil over his face..." Moses had done that when he felt Israel's commitment to their covenant was fading. Genesis 1:3 served Paul in 2 Corinthians 4:6:

> For God, who said, "Let light shine out of darkness," made his light shine in our hearts to give us the light of the knowledge of the glory of God in the face of Christ.

In warning new Christians not to yoke themselves with unbelievers in 2 Corinthians 6:16 Paul applied Leviticus 26:11–12:

> What agreement is there between the temple of God and idols? For we are the temple of the living God. As God has said: "I will live with them and walk among them, and I will be their God, and they will be my people."

In 2 Corinthians 8 Paul wrote about collecting donations for the needy in Jerusalem because famine had struck the area. The collection among the Macedonian churches had been generous, but the collection among the much richer Corinthians had stalled. To support his plea Paul noted Exodus 16:18, which addressed the distribution of manna in the desert during the time of Moses (2 Corinthians 8:15):

> as it is written: "He who gathered much did not have too much, and he who gathered little did not have too little."

Christians needed to share with another. In concluding 2 Corinthians Paul warned (13:1) the young church of his coming visit and subsequent discipline of sinning members, enlisting Deuteronomy 19:15, "Every matter must be established by the testimony of two or three witnesses." These were not the words of a man who did not believe the truth of the Law. Paul simply believed—as Jesus did—that the Law alone was not enough.

Paul's letter to the Galatians offered a splendid example of how thoroughly he thought in Scriptures. He wrote in Galatians 3:6–16 a succession of seven quotations from the Pentateuch (Genesis 15:6, Genesis 12:3, Deuteronomy 27:26, Habakkuk 2:4, Leviticus 18:5, Deuteronomy 21:23 and Genesis 12:7, all shown in italics):[31]

> Consider Abraham: *"He believed God, and it was credited to him as righteousness."* Understand, then, that those who believe are children of Abraham. The Scripture foresaw that God would justify the Gentiles by faith, and announced the gospel in advance to Abraham: *"All nations will be blessed through you."* So those who have faith are blessed along with Abraham, the man of faith.
>
> All who rely on observing the law are under a curse, for it is written: *"Cursed is everyone who does not continue to do everything written in the Book of the Law."* Clearly no one is justified before God by the law, because, *"The righteous will live by faith."* The law is not based on faith; on the contrary, *"The man who does these things will live by them."* Christ redeemed us from the curse of the law by becoming a curse for us, for it is written: *"Cursed is everyone who is hung on a tree."* He redeemed us in order that the blessing given to Abraham might come to the Gentiles through Christ Jesus, so that by faith we might receive the promise of the Spirit.
>
> Brothers, let me take an example from everyday life. Just as no one can set aside or add to a human covenant that has been duly established, so it is in this case. The promises were spoken to Abraham and to his seed. The Scripture does not say "and to seeds," meaning many people, but *"and to your seed,"* meaning one person, who is Christ.

Justification was by faith in Christ alone. The Law was added to the original covenant with Abraham and his descendants, yet it was a curse until Christ came. Note also how Paul tapped the Pentateuch for its Messianic prophecies.

Paul continued to make use of the Pentateuch in Galatians 4:30:

> But what does the Scripture say? "Get rid of the slave woman and her son, for the slave woman's son will never share in the inheritance with the free woman's son."

Here Paul cited Sarah's words in Genesis 21:10 to show the Galatians that they must cast aside the Jews who would deny Christ.

Lastly, in Galatians 5:13 Paul again employed Leviticus 19:18: "Love your neighbor as yourself." Genesis 2:24, which Paul applied in 1 Corinthians as becoming one flesh with Christ, served him again in the same sense in Ephesians 5:31. In Ephesians 6:2–3 Paul quoted Exodus 20:12: "Honor your father and mother that it may go well with you and that you may enjoy long life on the earth." In 1 Timothy 18 he once again cited Deuteronomy 25:4: "Do not muzzle the ox while it is treading out the grain." In 2 Timothy 2:19 he quoted a verse of Numbers 16:5 found only in the Septuagint: "Everyone who confesses the name of the Lord must turn away from wickedness."

Paul could summon the Pentateuch with ease. He called on it for many purposes. Paul quoted some passages in the Pentateuch for their Messianic prophecies. He also made use of the Pentateuch's authority to urge righteousness. Perhaps none of the other followers of Jesus articulated the attitude toward the Law as well as Paul did. He delighted in the Law, yet knew keeping the Law was not enough. Christ had changed all that.

Now consider how the other followers of Jesus loved the Pentateuch...

< 7 >

HOW OTHER FOLLOWERS OF JESUS LOVED THE 'LAW'

Note that this chapter details the 'Law' (or Pentateuch) as loved by the followers of Jesus — *other than Paul*. The exclusion of Paul will not be noted again (although his inclusion, if necessary, will be noted). The New Testament writers quoted the Pentateuch — or Moses' five books of the 'Law' — 27 times. This group includes New Testament letter writers as well as the writers of the narratives of Matthew, Mark, Luke, John and Acts.

WRITERS OF THE NEW TESTAMENT NARRATIVES

First, consider the writers of the narratives. Recall that quotes of the Pentateuch from the mouth of Jesus are not considered for the purpose here the narrative. Only Luke made use of quotations from the Pentateuch. This seems remarkable because the conventional opinion is that Luke catered to the Gentiles. Yet of all the narratives only his books — Luke and Acts — took direct quotes from the Pentateuch. Moreover Luke drew from the Pentateuch a total of 11 times (actually 13 times, counting the two quotes spoken by Paul and discussed in the previous chapter).

There is a reservation to this conclusion however. The Pentateuch was worked into the four Gospels not only though the narratives but through the words from Jesus. From that overall perspective, Matthew has six quotations, Mark eight, Luke 16 and John none. Perhaps the most remarkable conclusion then is that there is not one quotation from the Pentateuch in the Gospel of John.

Luke combined quotations of the Pentateuch (Exodus 13:2, also 13:12; and Leviticus 12:08) to show Jesus was officially consecrated to God at the Temple (in Luke 2:22–24):

> When the time of their purification according to the Law of Moses had been completed, Joseph and Mary took him to Jerusalem to present him to the Lord (as it is written in the Law of

31

the Lord, "Every firstborn male is to be consecrated to the Lord") and to offer a sacrifice in keeping with what is said in the Law of the Lord: "a pair of doves or two young pigeons."

Every use of the nine quotations from the Pentateuch in Luke's book of Acts occurred in speeches by the followers of Jesus to other Jews. The first occasion was when Peter spoke to the Jews at the Temple after Jesus had risen and ascended. Peter first made use of Deuteronomy 18:15–19, then Genesis 22:18, while explaining to the Jews that Jesus fulfilled the prophecies about the Messiah (Acts 3:22–25):

> For Moses said, 'The Lord your God will raise up for you a prophet like me from among your own people; you must listen to everything he tells you. Anyone who does not listen to him will be completely cut off from among his people.'
> Indeed, all the prophets from Samuel on, as many as have spoken, have foretold these days. And you are heirs of the prophets and of the covenant God made with your fathers. He said to Abraham, 'Through your offspring all peoples on earth will be blessed.'

How many today realize Moses himself uttered such a strong Messianic prophecy? Certainly Peter knew it after Jesus had risen and ascended. Because shortly after arising, Christ chastised Cleopas and another of his followers on the road to Emmaus. Christ scolded them for not appreciating the fact that Moses and all the prophets after Moses spoke of Christ in the Jewish Holy Scriptures. Luke recorded this revelation by Christ in Luke 24.

The rest of the direct quotations of the Pentateuch in the book of Acts were also in speeches — seven by Stephen (and two by Paul in the preceding chapter). Stephen defended himself against persecution from Jewish authorities by arguing from the Pentateuch. In Chapter 7 of Acts Luke recorded Stephen's long speech to the Sanhedrin, the Jewish council of religious leaders. Stephen's discourse on Jewish history was replete with allusions and direct quotes from the Pentateuch. In his summary of the history from Abraham to Moses he quoted Genesis 12:1, Genesis 15:13–14, Exodus 1:8, Exodus 2:13–14, Exodus 3:6, Exodus 32:1 and various phrases within Exodus 3:5–10. From the Jewish Holy Scriptures Stephen demonstrated how from Abraham to Jesus the Israelites had so often rejected their own prophets. He ended his speech by condemning the Jewish authorities for betraying Jesus. Enraged, they stoned him to death.

WRITERS OF THE NEW TESTAMENT LETTERS

Now consider the New Testament letter writers. They quoted the Pentateuch 16 times. Chief among them was the book to the Hebrews. This letter, aimed at Jewish converts, quoted the Old Testament 30 times, including the Pentateuch 11 times. The writer of Hebrews—an esteemed but unnamed follower of Jesus—revered the Old Testament but knew that Jesus started a new covenant. The theme of Hebrews was the absolute supremacy of Christ. In Hebrews 1:6 the writer quoted Deuteronomy 32:43 but not from the Masoretic text. He quoted a phrase—'Let all God's angels worship him'—found only in a manuscript of Deuteronomy among the Dead Sea Scrolls! Could the writer of the book of Hebrews have been an Essene, a member of the Jewish sect that is thought to have hidden the scrolls?

In chapters of the book of Hebrews that followed, the author occasionally cited the Pentateuch, usually in very short quotations, to support—much as Stephen did—his historical development of the Jews and the new covenant with Christ.

> And on the seventh day God rested from all his work.
> (Hebrews 4:4 from Genesis 2:2)

> I will surely bless you and give you many descendants.
> (Hebrews 6:14 from Genesis 22:17)

> See to it that you make everything according to the pattern shown you on the mountain.
> (Hebrews 8:5 from Exodus 25:40)

> This is the blood of the covenant that God has commanded you to keep.
> (Hebrews 9:20 from Exodus 24:8)

> It is mine to avenge; I will repay....
> (Hebrews 10:30a from Deuteronomy 32:35)

> The Lord will judge his people.
> (Hebrews 10:30b from Deuteronomy 32:36)

It is through Isaac that your offspring will be reckoned.
(Hebrews 11:18 from Genesis 21:12)

By faith Jacob, when he was dying, blessed each of Joseph's
    sons, and worshiped as he leaned on the top of his staff.
(Hebrews 11:21 from Genesis 47:31)

God is a consuming fire.
(Hebrews 12:29 from Deuteronomy 4:24)

Never will I leave you, never will I forsake you.
(Hebrews 13:5 from Deuteronomy 31:6)

The writer of the book of Hebrews methodically employed direct quotations of the Pentateuch through the book. The 11 passages were used as if to punctuate the author's argument with the authority of the Pentateuch. But the quotations also gave the argument a Jewish tone. Note that the writer of Hebrews did not neglect the mildly Messianic prophecy carried in Genesis 22:17.

James — the half-brother of Jesus — echoed this use of the Pentateuch as authority in his New Testament letter. All three of James' quotes of the Law of Moses occurred in the second chapter of his book. Most emphasized commandments: "Love your neighbor as yourself" (Leviticus 19:18 in James 2:8), "Do not commit adultery" and "Do not murder" (Exodus 20:13–14 in James 2:11). But one passage from Genesis 15:6, "Abraham believed God, and it was credited to him as righteousness," in James 2:23, preceded James' controversial statement of 2:24: "You see that a person is justified by what he does and not by faith alone."[32] The emphasis by James perhaps reflects a debate he had going on at the time with Paul.

The apostle Peter made use of the Pentateuch twice to emphasize holiness. In 1 Peter 1:16 he used God's words in Leviticus 11:44: "Be holy, because I am holy." In 1 Peter 2:9 he wrote "you are a chosen people, a royal priesthood, a holy nation...", a slight rewording of God's words in Exodus 19:6. Peter believed that the Christians were the chosen people in the new covenant (New Testament), just as the Jews were God's chosen people in the old covenants (Old Testament).

In summary, New Testament writers drew from the Pentateuch for their own particular purposes. Like Jesus and Paul, they often quoted the Pentateuch for authority. They urged righteousness. They also cited the Pentateuch for quoting speeches accurately, for historical support, and a Jewish tone. And though the Pentateuch was scarcely rich in Messianic prophecy, the New Testament writers (including Paul) did quote some of those passages. Yes, it was important to remind Jews that the great patriarch Moses himself foresaw the Messiah.

This chapter and the previous three chapters only considered the Pentateuch (or Law). The Pentateuch was the source of one-third of the Old Testament quotes in the New Testament.

Much yet remains to be considered...

< 8 >

MESSAGE OF THE PSALMS IN THE 'WRITINGS'

Jesus and his followers quoted the book of Psalms 60 times in the New Testament. That amount is nearly one-fourth of the total of 247. This preference is astonishing, even though no book in the Old Testament (or the New Testament) is larger than the book of Psalms. Nevertheless the book of Psalms is only 10 percent of the Old Testament, yet it accounts for 25 percent of the quotations of the Old Testament in the New Testament. Why did Jesus and his followers so love the book of Psalms? What was its message?

The book of Psalms is a collection of hymns to God and about God. Many scholars believe the ancient Jews used psalms in the rituals of the synagogues, perhaps not too unlike Jews today use psalms in synagogues. Tradition credited King David with writing the Psalms. Notations on the Psalms themselves in ancient manuscripts[33] specifically attributed 73 of the 150 psalms to David. But not even the ancients believed he wrote all of them. In fact, one was attributed to Moses, who died about 400 years before King David's reign began in 1010 BC. But the Psalms surely reflect heightened dialogue between God and his chosen people in times of turmoil and triumph. And surely no time after Moses and before Christ was as full of turmoil and triumph as King David's unification of the nation.[34]

Modern liberal scholarship has tended to discredit David's authorship of any psalm.[35] Such an approach defies Biblical evidence that David was a gifted poet and musician. Such an approach defies the fact that David's great song of thanksgiving in 2 Samuel 22:2–51 is also Psalm 18. Both begin "The Lord is my rock, my fortress and my deliverer" and end many verses later with "He gives his king great victories; he shows unfailing kindness to his anointed, to David and his descendants forever."

Did Jesus and his followers speak of David's authorship of psalms? Most definitely. Jesus in Mark 12:6 (also Matthew 22:43, Luke

20:42) left no doubt David was the author of Psalm 110. Peter in Acts 1:16–20 specifically attributed Psalms 69 and 109 to David. Later in Acts 2:25–28 and Acts 2:34–35 Peter added Psalms 16 and 110 to David's authorship. In Acts 4:25–26 Peter and John attested to Psalm 2 coming from David's mouth by the Holy Spirit. In Romans 6–8 Paul credited David with Psalm 32. In Romans 11:9–10 Paul imputed Psalm 69 to David. Moreover, Hebrews 4:7 cited David as the author of Psalm 95. There is little doubt Jesus and his followers thought David wrote several psalms through the Holy Spirit.

The book of Psalms has five divisions, each with its last psalm ending in a doxology — that is, one or more couplets in praise of God. Consensus today among conservative scholars concludes that Books 1 and 2, which contain Psalms 1 to 72, date from the age of David. Many of these psalms probably were from David's genius. Though Books 3 through 5 — or, Psalms 73 to 150 — also have psalms attributed to David, many of the psalms may have been added later, perhaps several hundred years later.

Some scholars believe the five books represent different collections of psalms that circulated at various times in Israel's history. The ancients at some time combined the five collections into the book of Psalms that persists today. The truth may be that arbitrary. After all, psalms attributed to David appear in all five sections. Also, different types of psalms appear in all five sections, suggesting each section within itself might once have been considered a complete collection — comparable to a hymnal. Whatever the origin of the five sections, the presence of the book of Psalms among the Dead Sea Scrolls confirmed something important. The book of Psalms that Jesus and his followers loved was virtually identical with the book of Psalms of today.

Many scholars have attempted to classify the varieties of psalms. German theologian Hermann Gunkel (1862–1932) was one of the first to classify psalms by form and intent. The recent classification in the same vein by Gordon Fee and Douglas Stuart is widely used.[36] They distinguish seven categories with numerous subcategories. Chief among their main categories is that of laments. Laments number more than 60 of the 150 psalms. Laments are loud, emotional outpourings of grief. Rather than depressing their mourners, laments help them articulate their sorrow, vent their grief and subsequently heal. A lament may be 'individual' in that it expresses personal grief. Or it may be 'corporate' in that it grieves for groups or the nation of Israel.

Celebration/Affirmation psalms, a second category, number 26 in all. These seem liturgical, as if they affirmed the onset of kings and the holiness of Jerusalem. Fee and Stuart break them down further into nine 'Royal' psalms, nine 'Enthronement' psalms, six 'Songs of Zion' or 'Jerusalem' and two 'covenant renewal liturgies'. A third category by Fee and Stuart groups psalms expressing gratitude to God. These 'thanksgiving' psalms — about 16 — are the opposite of laments. But like laments, thanksgiving psalms may be 'individual' or 'corporate'. Close in intent is the fourth category, 'Hymns of Praise', also numbering about 16. These psalms praise God. They are focused, with no apparent direction to either disappointment or happiness. They praise God as 'Master of History', 'Protector of Israel' and 'Creator'.

Fee and Stuart recognize three other categories of psalms, each including ten or less. 'Songs of Trust' tout the theme: God can be trusted. Psalms of 'Wisdom' are almost 'proverbial', a euphemism for sayings of a relatively secular nature. 'Salvation History Psalms' are of a sweeping character, reviewing God's deliverance of the Jews. Derek Kidner[37] mentions another special kind of psalm: penitential. These seven psalms (6, 32, 38, 51, 102, 130 and 143) he characterizes as mainly confessing sins.

The classification of Fee and Stuart is not exact. Some psalms fit two classes. Psalm 18 seems equally valid as a thanksgiving psalm or as a royal psalm. Psalm 144 seems valid as a royal psalm or as a lament. About 10 psalms are more distinguished by their cursing (hexing, not swearing) than their category of laments. They are often called 'imprecations', a word synonymous with curses or hexes. Psalm 137 is universally regarded a problem with its barbaric hex against the Edomites in verses 8 and 9:

> O Daughter of Babylon, doomed to destruction, happy is he
> who repays you for what you have done to us —
> he who seizes your infants and dashes them against the rocks.

How can such a cruel curse against the Edomites be defended? Its intense rancor can only be understood — but not justified — in historical context. Edomites aided Babylonians in their destruction of Jerusalem and the Temple. The Jews were subsequently held decades captive in Babylon. Not only did the Edomites rejoice at the humiliation of the Jews but they took advantage of the captivity of the Jews in Babylon by settling in Israel as far north as Hebron. Psalm 137 was written in the frustration of captivity. Are 2500 years of separation from these events too many to feel the agony and anger of the captive Jews?

Also, scholars distinguish many psalms not by the intent Fee and Stuart emphasized but by their Messianic content. Such Messianic psalms are included within nearly every category of Fee and Stuart. Derek Kidner lists 15 Messianic psalms.[38] Scholar John Walvoord, whose specific aim was to find prophecy, lists 29 Messianic psalms.[39] *Eerdmans Handbook to the Bible* lists 11 Messianic psalms.[40] Such a wide range in the number of Messianic psalms reveals that recognizing prophecy of the Messiah in the Jewish Holy Scriptures is not an exact science. Kidner notes that the followers of Jesus often recognized passages in psalms as Messianic that suggest nothing at all about the Messiah to today's reader.[41] Luke 24:45 explained that just before ascending to heaven Jesus 'opened their [his followers] minds so they could understand the Scriptures.'

One more preliminary consideration of Psalms is necessary. This element was emphasized by popular writer C. S. Lewis: the psalms are poems.[42] They were even poems meant to be sung. They should not be regarded as doctrinal treatises or sermons.[43] Because they were the very best kind of Jewish poetry they were full of imagery and hyperbole (or exaggeration). They used emotional connections rather than logical connections. One can not fathom the true meaning in the psalms if one does not appreciate that they are poetry.

The meter of Jewish poetry was not parceled out in 'feet' or a prescribed arrangement of strong and weak syllables. Stresses could vary, with the commonest rhythm 3:3. A 3:2 rhythm suited laments because of a falling cadence. Stanzas varied and they are often hard to define at all. The feature that truly distinguished Hebrew poetry is the 'parallelism'. The lines of poetry represent thoughts. 'Line one' expresses a thought; the next line or two answers that thought. Often the answer is synonymous, simply reinforcing the first line. But a long succession of such couplets is tedious. So the answering line or lines can be 'antithetic', or in opposition. The mind holds strongly to parallelism. Who can forget the simple 'Old King Cole was a merry old soul, and a merry old soul was he!'? Fortunately, the nature of Hebrew poetry also lends itself very suitably to translation.

But how did Jesus and his followers love this ancient poetry directed to God? That is considered next…

< 9 >

HOW JESUS LOVED PSALMS

Jesus appealed to the Psalms no fewer than 10 times, about one-fourth of his quotes from Old Testament books. He quoted the Psalms in all situations: to hostile Jewish authorities, to sympathetic crowds, and to his disciples in private. It was no more obvious how much he loved the Psalms than during his agony on the cross. Of his seven recorded utterances on the cross, two were quotes from the Old Testament and both were Psalms.

Psalm 22:1 was the source for the last words of Jesus recorded by Mark (Mark 15:34):

> And at the ninth hour Jesus cried out in a loud voice, "Eloi, Eloi, lama sabachthani?" — which means, "My God, my God, why have you forsaken me?"

Psalm 22 was a lament for an individual in agony. But it was strongly Messianic. No experience of David's can explain it; it clearly lamented suffering during an execution. The crucifixion fulfilled many verses of Psalm 22. Verse 16 of Psalm 22 said, "they have pierced my hands and my feet". Verse 18 cried, 'they cast lots for my clothing'. Verse 7 said, "All who see me mock me; they hurl insults, shaking their heads'. Verse 8 lamented that they mocked him with the words, "he trusts in the Lord; let the Lord rescue him'. Is it any wonder Jesus cried out the first verse of Psalm 22? In agony he affirmed he was the Messiah.

Luke 23:46 recorded Jesus drawing on Psalm 31:5 as he died on the cross:

> Jesus called out with a loud voice, "Father, into your hands I commit my spirit." When he had said this, he breathed his last.

Psalm 31 was also a lament for individuals, probably written by David during or after one of his harrowing adventures. Some conservative scholars believe David wrote the psalm when he was in the wilderness of Ziph, after being betrayed by King Saul. It is not choked with Messianic meaning as is Psalm 22, but still it was significant. The remainder of verse 5 — "redeem me, O Lord, the God of truth" — Jesus did not utter. After all, he is the Redeemer.

As noted above, Jesus often quoted psalms in response to questions, both well-intentioned and hostile. Three of these occasions involved hostile questions. One incident was at the Temple when the 'chief priests and teachers of the law' were outraged that children were chanting, "Hosanna to the Son of David." Matthew 21:16 recorded that in response to their indignation Jesus made use of Psalm 8:2:

> "Yes," replied Jesus, "have you never read, 'From the lips of children and infants you have ordained praise'?"

Psalm 8 was a hymn of praise for the Creator. God allied himself with the weakest of the weak, 'children and infants'. Jesus quoted the first half of verse 2 at the Temple not only to affirm he was Messiah but to acknowledge his detractors. The chief priests and teachers of the law knew only too well the second half of the verse that Jesus had left unspoken: 'because of your enemies, to silence the foe and the avenger'.

In Mark 12, in the presence of a crowd at the Temple, Jesus directed the parable of the tenants to the chief priests, teachers of the law and elders. Then he asked them if they had read Psalm 118:22–23 (in Mark 12:10–11):

> Haven't you read this scripture: 'The stone the builders rejected has become the capstone; the Lord has done this, and it is marvelous in our eyes'?

Psalm 118 was not only an individual psalm of thanksgiving, but clearly that of a king. Once rejected, the king in the psalm was now victorious against many nations, thanks to God. By applying this psalm Jesus acknowledged to all — including the chief priests, teachers of the law and elders — that he considered himself the Messiah. Only fear of the crowd kept the Jewish authorities from arresting him.

John recorded another confrontation at the Temple. The Jewish authorities threatened to stone Jesus for blasphemy because he, a mere man, claimed to be God. Jesus responded with Psalm 82:6 (in John 10:34), which involved God's eventual judgment on unjust rulers and judges:

> Jesus answered them, "Is it not written in your Law, 'I have said you are gods'? If he called them 'gods,' to whom the word of

> God came — and the Scripture cannot be broken — what about
> the one whom the Father set apart as his very own and sent into
> the world? Why then do you accuse me of blasphemy because I
> said, 'I am God's Son'?"

Once again an unspoken portion of a verse added weight to his argument, for the rest of Psalm 82:6 read 'you are all sons of the Most
High'. How then could anyone calling himself the 'Son of God' blaspheme? Again Jesus stymied the Jews in authority with the greater
authority of Scripture. Before the befuddled authorities could resolve
the question among themselves Jesus had vanished.

On yet another occasion at the Temple, recorded in Mark 12:35–
37, Jesus raised the paradox of Psalm 110:1:

> While Jesus was teaching in the temple courts, he asked, "How
> is it that the teachers of the law say that the Christ is the son of
> David? David himself, speaking by the Holy Spirit, declared:
>> The Lord said to my Lord: 'Sit at my right hand until I put
>> your enemies under your feet.'
> David himself calls him 'Lord.' How then can he be his son?"

Mark went on to write that the large crowd at the Temple listened to
Jesus with delight. But not delighted were the chief priests, teachers of
the law and elders who were also listening. Psalm 110 was a royal
psalm that went beyond being strongly Messianic. The paradox indicated the Messiah was divine.

The remaining four occasions involved Jesus quoting Psalms to
listeners who were mainly sympathetic. Near the end of the Sermon
on the Mount, lamenting that some would reject his message that represented the will of the Father, Jesus very emotionally recalled Psalm
6:8 (Matthew 7:23):

> Then I will tell them plainly, 'I never knew you. Away from me,
> you evildoers!'

Psalm 6 was indeed anguished, a lament but also one of Derek
Kidner's seven 'penitential psalms'. Some conservative scholars believe David wrote Psalm 6 after Nathan rebuked him for his sinful behavior with Bathsheba and Uriah. It was not Messianic but contained
the degree of anguish — and even anger — Jesus felt at the thought of
lost souls.

In John 13:18–19, at the Last Supper, Jesus made use of Psalm 41:9 to indicate not only that one of the disciples would betray him but also that the betrayal was inevitable because Jesus was the Messiah:

> But this is to fulfill the scripture: 'He who shares my bread has lifted up his heel against me.' I am telling you now before it happens, so that when it does happen you will believe that I am He…

Psalm 41 was an individual lament. Many believe David wrote it, once again after Nathan rebuked him for his sinful behavior with Bathsheba and Uriah. Nevertheless it was definitely Messianic.

Again in the book of John, while Jesus was speaking to those at the Last Supper he indicated he was the Messiah fulfilling Scripture. He cited Psalm 35:19 (in John 15:25):

> If I had not done among them what no one else did, they would not be guilty of sin. But now they have seen these miracles, and yet they have hated both me and my Father. But this is to fulfill what is written in their Law: 'They hated me without reason.'

Psalm 35 was an imprecatory or cursing lament of some notoriety. Its author was being viciously slandered and mocked by those he loved. This may have been written by David after King Saul tried to murder him. His flight was just beginning. Many gloated over his distress. All this bitter disappointment Jesus summoned in his quote. Again it was not just one convenient line Jesus drew upon but the entire effect of the psalm.

The last quote of Psalms by Jesus occurred in John's Revelation. Psalm 2:9 served Jesus in John's vision (Revelations 2:26–27):

> To him who overcomes and does my will to the end, I will give authority over the nations—'He will rule them with an iron scepter; he will dash them to pieces like pottery'—just as I have received authority from my Father.

Psalm 2 was a royal psalm, very definitely Messianic. It was notable that the quote was from the Septuagint, in which the Greek text said he will 'rule them', rather than from the Masoretic Hebrew text, which said he will 'break them'.

In summary, the ten quotations of Psalms by Jesus revealed an intimate knowledge of the Psalms. Most of the psalms he employed were considered Messianic. However, he used them in a variety of situations. The usage was masterful. Just a few words might have been quoted, yet they drew forth a much larger meaning — or a much larger emotion — that suited the occasion.

Next, consider how Paul loved the psalms...

< 10 >

HOW PAUL LOVED PSALMS

Paul quoted Psalms 22 times in his writings and in Acts. Consider this astonishing fact: of all those 22 quotes he only twice used the same psalms that Jesus quoted. And even on those two occasions he did not make use of the same verses. Paul and Jesus both quoted Psalm 2. In Acts 13:32-33 Paul quotes Psalm 2:7:

> We tell you the good news: What God promised our fathers he has fulfilled for us, their children, by raising up Jesus. As it is written in the second Psalm: 'You are my Son; today I have become your Father.'

Psalm 2 was one of the 'royal' psalms, and quite Messianic. Paul employed it with many other Scriptural quotations in his argument to the Jews in the synagogue at Antioch in Pisidia. Although Paul did not make use of the same verse as Jesus his intended message was the same: Jesus was the Messiah.

The second psalm Paul quoted that Jesus also quoted was Psalm 8, of which Paul analyzed verse 6 in 1 Corinthians 15:27:

> For he "has put everything under his feet." Now when it says that "everything" has been put under him, it is clear that this does not include God himself, who put everything under Christ.

Psalm 8 was a psalm praising God as the Creator. Paul used it to speak of end times. Everything under 'his feet' in 1 Corinthians 15 included the destruction of the Satanic 'dominion, authority and power', and lastly the destruction of 'death'. Paul's intended message was unlike the message intended by Jesus when he quoted the psalm.

The only 'same Psalm, same verse' that Paul shared with the other followers of Jesus was Psalm 69:9, which John also quoted. But John applied the first half of the verse. For a totally different purpose Paul used the second half in Romans 15:3: 'The insults of those who insult you have fallen on me.' Psalm 69 was an imprecation, or angry cursing psalm, that pleaded with God for justice. But the psalm was also strongly Messianic. Because of that, any use of a quote from Psalm 69 also carried the expectation of the Messiah. In Paul's context, verse 9 of Psalm 69 meant not only that Christ bore the insults that were intended for God but also that the good Christian must bear the insults intended for his weaker brothers.

Paul made use of Psalm 69 a second time, this time verses 22 and 23, in Romans 11:9–10:

> And David says:
> "May their table become a snare and a trap, a stumbling block and a retribution for them.
> May their eyes be darkened so they cannot see, and their backs be bent forever."

Verses 22 and 23 of strongly Messianic Psalm 69 were used much like the often-quoted Isaiah 6:9–10 with its 'ever hearing, but never understanding, ever seeing, but never perceiving' message. God would protect his faithful by hindering the senses of their enemies.

In the four preceding quotes, Paul did not actually use the same passages of Psalms used by Jesus and his other followers. As a result, every one of the 22 quotes of the Psalms by Paul in the New Testament is unique. Now consider the remaining 18 quotations of Psalms by Paul.

In his argument with the Jews in the synagogue at Antioch in Pisidia Paul quoted another psalm. Luke recorded Paul employing Psalm 16:10 in Acts 13:35:

> So it is stated elsewhere: 'You will not let your Holy One see decay.'

Paul's purpose here was to emphasize that Jesus was the Holy One prophesied in the Scriptures. The Holy One was not David. David was buried. His body decayed. By Jewish custom, relatives later gathered his bones and deposited them in an ossuary. But Paul brought his listeners good news that this had never happened with the real Holy One, who was Jesus. He had risen! He was the Messiah.

Psalms served Paul 10 times in the book of Romans (six of those in the third chapter on righteousness). In Romans 2:6 Paul made use of Psalm 62:12: God "will give to each person according to what he has done." Psalm 62 was a song of Thanksgiving. Paul used it to show justice is ultimately rendered by God.[44]

In Romans 3:4 Paul cited Psalm 51:4:

> As it is written: "So that you may be proved right when you speak and prevail when you judge."

Psalm 51 was one of the penitential psalms mentioned by Kidner. The verse was meant as an irony: if sin was good for nothing else it was good in that it proved God was right and God would prevail.

In verses 12 through 18 of Romans 3, Paul, using the rabbinic technique called 'charaz', strung together a succession of quotes from five Psalms and one passage from Isaiah (Isaiah 59:7–8: 'Their feet are swift...they do not know' was the fifth of the six quotes that follow):

> As it is written: 'There is no one righteous, not even one; there is no one who understands, no one who seeks God.
> All have turned away, they have together become worthless; there is no one who does good, not even one.'
> 'Their throats are open graves; their tongues practice deceit.'
> 'The poison of vipers is on their lips.'
> 'Their mouths are full of cursing and bitterness.'
> 'Their feet are swift to shed blood; ruin and misery mark their ways, and the way of peace they do not know.'
> 'There is no fear of God before their eyes.'

Except for the passage from Isaiah, the five Psalms — each set off by quotation marks — were in succession: 14:3, 5:9, 140:3, 10:7 and 36:1. All these psalms condemned sinners. Paul's point here was that neither Jews nor Gentiles were righteous under the Law. All were in sin. Yet all could be saved by faith in Christ.

Paul applied Psalm 32:1–2 in Romans 4:7–8:

> 'Blessed are they whose transgressions are forgiven, whose sins are covered.
> Blessed is the man whose sin the Lord will never count against him.'

Psalm 32, a psalm of individual thanksgiving, was cited by Paul as evidence God credited faith as righteousness. Of course Paul and other believers knew their sins were paid for by Christ.

In Romans 8:36 Paul made use of Psalm 44:22:

As it is written: 'For your sake we face death all day long; we are considered as sheep to be slaughtered.'

Psalm 44, a corporate lament, enlarged on Paul's question in Romans 8:35: 'Who shall separate us from Christ?' Paul insisted Christians would persevere.

Psalm 19:4 aided Paul in Romans 10:8:

But what does it say? "The word is near you; it is in your mouth and in your heart," that is, the word of faith we are proclaiming:

With Psalm 19, which praised the Creator, Paul introduced verse 9, his inspired formula for salvation: 'That if you confess with your mouth, "Jesus is Lord," and believe in your heart that God raised him from the dead, you will be saved.'

Psalm 117:1 Paul used in Romans 15:11:

'Praise the Lord, all you Gentiles, and sing praises to him, all you peoples.'

Psalm 117 praised God as master of history and urged everyone to sing praises. It was one of a succession of Old Testament passages Paul quoted to prove salvation was intended for Gentiles as well as Jews.

Paul employed Psalm 94:11 in his first letter to the Corinthians (3:20) in Greece: 'The Lord knows that the thoughts of the wise are futile.' Although Psalm 94, a corporate lament, wanted punishment for the wicked, part of it refuted the futility (and arrogance) of human wisdom. Paul applied it for the same purpose. The Greeks were famously vain about their 'learning' and philosophy.

In the same letter Paul quoted Psalm 24:1 (1 Corinthians 10:26): 'The earth is the Lord's, and everything in it.' Paul used Psalm 24 — an enthronement type of the celebration/affirmation psalm — to show believers the Old Covenant restrictions on eating had ended. All bounty came from God. Why should the recipients of this bounty not eat what they wanted?

In his second letter to the Corinthians Paul cited Psalm 116:10 (in the first verse of 2 Corinthians 4:13–14):

It is written: "I believed; therefore I have spoken." With that same spirit of faith we also believe and therefore speak, because we know that the one who raised the Lord Jesus from the dead will also raise us with Jesus and present us with you in his presence.

Psalm 116 was a song of individual thanksgiving. The verse meant that faith leads to speaking out: in distress as in Psalm 116 itself, or in testimony of Jesus in Paul's case.

Psalm 112:9 Paul used in 2 Corinthians 9:9:

'He has scattered abroad his gifts to the poor; his righteousness endures forever.'

Paul employed Psalm 112, a psalm of wisdom, to urge believers to give, or 'sow', generously. In that way they themselves would reap righteousness.

Paul applied Psalm 68:18 in Ephesians 4:8:

'When he ascended on high, he led captives in his train and gave gifts to men.'

Paul's immediate purpose in using this psalm of celebration for God's triumph and generosity was to explain that through Christ's grace the believers also received varying gifts.

Paul began Ephesians 4:26-27 by quoting Psalm 4:4:

'In your anger do not sin': Do not let the sun go down while you are still angry, and do not give the devil a foothold.

Paul used this psalm of David that urged righteousness as part of his instructions to live in righteousness and holiness.

The preceding 22 quotations certainly show how Paul loved the Psalms. Most often he quoted them to counsel his churches scattered around the Mediterranean. And what was his message? Paul wanted his churches to know keeping the law was not enough for justification. Faith in Christ was enough. He also quoted the Psalms to stress righteousness, for he urged believers to live a life of righteousness until Christ came again. Only occasionally however did Paul use the psalms to indicate Jesus was the Messiah.

Next consider how the other writers of the New Testament loved the Psalms...

< 11 >

HOW OTHER FOLLOWERS OF JESUS LOVED PSALMS

Note again: this chapter details the Psalms as loved by the followers of Jesus — *other than Paul*. How well did the followers of Jesus love the book of Psalms? They quoted the Psalms 28 times. Once again, consider the use of Psalms in relation to its use by Jesus. Five times the followers of Jesus quoted the same Psalm, same verse that Jesus quoted. John in Revelations 19:15 made use of Psalm 2:9, which stated 'He will rule them with an iron scepter'. Peter at the Pentecost in Acts 2:34–35 cited Psalm 110:1, which related the enigma of David saying 'The Lord said to my Lord'. The writer of Hebrews quoted the same enigma of Psalm 110:1 in Hebrews 1:13. Peter, before the Sanhedrin in Acts 4:11, used Psalm 118:22, which lamented the builders rejecting the stone that later became the capstone. In 1 Peter 2:7 he once again employed Psalm 118:22. Jesus and his followers clearly loved Psalms 2, 110 and 118. All three psalms are strongly Messianic.

On 10 occasions the followers of Jesus quoted the same Psalm as Jesus but a different verse. Again Psalm 2 was prominent. The writer of Hebrews used Psalm 2:7 (as had Paul in the book of Acts) and its pointed 'You are my Son; today I have become your Father' in both Hebrews 1:5 and 5:5. Also Peter and John raised their voices together in Acts 4:25–26 to quote Psalm 2:1–2 to their followers:

> You spoke by the Holy Spirit through the mouth of your servant, our father David:
> 'Why do the nations rage and the peoples plot in vain?
> The kings of the earth take their stand and the rulers gather together against the Lord and against his Anointed One.'

Another psalm that both Jesus and his followers made use of is Psalm 8. Hebrews 2:6–8 quoted Psalm 8:4–6:

> But there is a place where someone has testified:

> "What is man that you are mindful of him, the son of man that you care for him?
> You made him a little lower than the angels; you crowned him with glory and honor and put everything under his feet."

Psalm 8 is a psalm praising God as the Creator. Paul had also quoted verse 6. The writer of Hebrews followed the quote by pointing out that although God ordained man to have everything on earth under his feet, that promised dominion remained unfulfilled — until the advent of the sinless Christ.

The very Messianic Psalm 22, an individual lament, elicited Christ's suffering words on the cross. Psalm 22:18 was quoted both in Matthew 27:35 and John 19:24 to prove prophesy had been fulfilled at the crucifixion. The latter of the two read:

> This happened that the Scripture might be fulfilled, which said: They divided my garments among them and cast lots for my clothing.

John, an eyewitness to the crucifixion, recorded that four Roman soldiers divided up all the clothing of Jesus — except his long undergarment. They did indeed cast lots for the undergarment.

Hebrews 2:12 employed Psalm 22:22:

> I will declare your name to my brothers; in the presence of the congregation I will sing your praises.

Here the writer invoked the psalm to invite one and all to sing praise to the Savior who suffered so much for them.

Verse 4 of Psalm 110, the Messianic psalm discussed above, is quoted by the writer of Hebrews in Hebrews 5:6: "You are a priest forever, in the order Melchizedek." Hebrews noted the special status of Melchizedek, the mysterious priest/king of Genesis, to emphasize that only Jesus the Messiah fulfilled that role.

Mark used verse 26 of Psalm 118, also discussed above, in Mark 11:9: 'Blessed is he who comes in the name of the lord!' Psalm 118 is not only an individual psalm of thanksgiving but also clearly that of a king. Mark employed it for the triumphal entrance of Jesus into Jerusalem for Passover.

Hebrews 13:6 made use of Psalm 118:6–7:

The Lord is my helper; I will not be afraid. What can man do to me?

The writer of Hebrews seemed often to delve into a different aspect of a Messianic Psalm. Psalm 118 is noted for its Messianic revelation that the builders rejected the stone that later became the capstone. Here the writer of Hebrews used it to encourage fellow Christians.

The previous discussion demonstrated that Jesus and his followers were particularly fond of Psalms 2, 8, 22, 110 and 118. Now consider the psalms quoted by followers of Jesus that were not also quoted by Jesus. First among these was Psalm 69, an imprecatory psalm that carried considerable anger. Not only did both Peter and John make use of it but Paul used it twice in Romans. In Acts 1:20 Peter recited Psalm 69:25 angrily against Judas:

May his place be deserted; let there be no one to dwell in it.

In a completely different context, John 2:17 employed Psalm 69:9:

His disciples remembered that it is written: "Zeal for your house will consume me."

The quote acknowledged Jesus driving the money-changers out of the Temple. John's account did not specifically say Jesus was angry, but the nature of Psalm 69 suggested to any Jew that Jesus was angry.

Psalm 34 ranked second among psalms quoted by New Testament writers that were not also quoted by Jesus. Both Peter and John made use of it. Peter used Psalm 34:12–16 in 1 Peter 3:10–12:

Whoever would love life and see good days must keep his tongue from evil and his lips from deceitful speech.
He must turn from evil and do good; he must seek peace and pursue it.
For the eyes of the Lord are on the righteous and his ears are attentive to their prayer, but the face of the Lord is against those who do evil.

Peter (as he often did in his letters) used a quote to emphasize righteousness, not to prove Jesus was the Messiah.

Yet John used the same psalm to add another prophecy Jesus had fulfilled. John saw the Roman soldiers break the legs of the other two on the crosses to hasten their deaths. But the soldiers did not do that to Jesus. He was already dead. So John 19:36 recalled Psalm 34:20:

> These things happened so that the scripture would be fulfilled:
> "Not one of his bones will be broken..."

Yet Psalm 34 is not generally considered Messianic, but a very popular psalm of individual thanksgiving.

A psalm quoted once by followers of Jesus is Psalm 16. Peter cited Psalm 16:8–11 in Acts 2:25–28:

> David said about him:
>> 'I saw the Lord always before me.
>> Because he is at my right hand, I will not be shaken.
>> Therefore my heart is glad and my tongue rejoices; my body also will live in hope, because you will not abandon me to the grave, nor will you let your Holy One see decay.
>> You have made known to me the paths of life; you will fill me with joy in your presence.'

In Acts Paul also applied this psalm to emphasize the fact that Jesus had risen. He was the 'Holy One'. King David, the author of Psalm 16, had decayed in a grave in Jerusalem.

Now consider those psalms whose quotes by followers of Jesus are unique in the New Testament. Three occur in the gospels. One is Psalm 78:2, used in Matthew 13:35:

> So was fulfilled what was spoken through the prophet: "I will open my mouth in parables, I will utter things hidden since the creation of the world."

Matthew referred to the prophet Asaph, author of Psalm 78, one of only five Psalms classified as 'salvation history' by Fee and Stuart. Matthew recorded Jesus speaking to friendly crowds around the Sea of Galilee, although hostile Jewish authorities were there too. The parables Jesus told revealed their secrets to the faithful. Unbelievers understood nothing.

Luke 4:10–11 recorded Psalm 91:11–12:

> For it is written:
> 'He will command his angels concerning you to guard you carefully; they will lift you up in their hands, so that you will not strike your foot against a stone.'

Believe it or not, Satan employed this psalm, trying to tempt Jesus — and thus abort his great mission. Psalm 91 was a song of trust in God.

But Satan used it deceitfully. God protects those faithful who serve and sacrifice, not those selfish who want to gain advantage.

Psalm 109:8 Peter used in Acts 1:20: 'May another take his place of leadership.' Peter referred to Judas, the betrayer of Jesus. Implied too was the first half of verse, 'May his days be few' — and thank God for that. Psalm 109 was well-known for its anger and cursing. So it was no surprise Peter used it on the subject of Judas.

Peter was also the only one who made use of Psalm 55. In 1 Peter 5:7 he wrote: 'Cast all your anxiety on him because he cares for you.' Psalm 55:22 was part of an appeal to the young men of the new churches to be submissive, humble and self-controlled. Peter followed this appeal with a warning that the devil prowled around like a lion looking for victims.

The final five unique quotes of psalms were all found in the book of Hebrews. Verses 7 through 12 of the first chapter of Hebrews employed three Psalms — 104:4, 45:6-7 and 102:25-27 — in succession:

> In speaking of the angels he (God) says,
>   "He makes his angels winds, his servants flames of fire."
> But about the Son he says,
>   "Your throne, O God, will last for ever and ever, and right-
>   eousness will be the scepter of your kingdom.
>   You have loved righteousness and hated wickedness; there-
>   fore God, your God, has set you above your companions
>   by anointing you with the oil of joy."
> He also says,
>   "In the beginning, O Lord, you laid the foundations of the
>   earth, and the heavens are the work of your hands.
>   They will perish, but you remain; they will all wear out like
>   a garment.
>   You will roll them up like a robe; like a garment they will be
>   changed.
>   But you remain the same, and your years will never end."

The writer of Hebrews quoted the psalms to prove Christ's supremacy over the angels. The first, Psalm 104, is a corporate praise psalm. The last, Psalm 102, is also corporate praise, but it was one of Kidner's 'penitential' psalms as well. Neither of these two psalms is strongly Messianic. However the psalm in the middle, Psalm 45, is a royal psalm and strongly Messianic.

Psalm 95 also occurred uniquely in the book of Hebrews, although it was used there five different times! The most complete quote of Psalms 95:7–11 was in Hebrews 3:7–11:

> Today, if you hear his voice, do not harden your hearts as you did in the rebellion, during the time of testing in the desert, where your fathers tested and tried me and for forty years saw what I did.
>
> That is why I was angry with that generation, and I said, 'Their hearts are always going astray, and they have not known my ways.'
>
> So I declared on oath in my anger, 'They shall never enter my rest.'

Psalm 95 is a special kind of celebration/affirmation hymn called an enthronement psalm. The writer of Hebrews repeatedly quoted Psalm 95 to emphasize that Israel repeatedly rejected God. Yet the opportunity still remained for people to accept Christ and enter God's 'rest'.

Psalm 40:6–8 in Hebrews 10:5–7 is the last unique occurrence of a psalm in the book of Hebrews:

> Therefore, when Christ came into the world, he said:
> "Sacrifice and offering you did not desire, but a body you prepared for me; with burnt offerings and sin offerings you were not pleased.
> Then I said, 'Here I am—it is written about me in the scroll—I have come to do your will, O God.'"

Psalm 40, an individual thanksgiving psalm, is astonishingly Messianic, especially the last verse quoted above.

The New Testament writers (other than Paul) quoted 17 psalms a total of 28 times. The six psalms they loved most account for 17 of the quotations. Certainly of these six favorites, the writers favored no particular category of psalms (in the classification of Fee and Stuart). Two (22, 69) are laments; two (2, 110) are celebration/affirmation psalms; and two (34, 118) are hymns of thanksgiving. Derek Kidner considers all of them but Psalm 34 strongly Messianic.[45] Of all 17 psalms quoted by the followers of Jesus other than Paul, Kidner considers 11 of them Messianic. These 11 Messianic psalms accounted for 19 of the 28 quotations. Clearly, like Jesus, (but in contrast to Paul) the New Testament writers employed psalms mainly for their Messianic impact.

Now consider the message of the prophet Isaiah…

< 12 >

MESSAGE OF ISAIAH IN THE 'PROPHETS'

Jesus and his followers quoted the book of Isaiah 56 times in the New Testament. That number approaches one-fourth of the total 247. This is an astonishing preference. Yes, the book is large — about 37,000 words — but still less than seven percent of the Old Testament. Yet it accounts for nearly 23 percent of the quotations of the Old Testament in the New Testament. Why did Jesus and his followers so love the book of Isaiah? What was the message of the prophet Isaiah?

First, consider the nature of Isaiah's voluminous book. Isaiah lived 200 years after the death of David's successor Solomon. The kingdom of Israel had peaked under the reigns of David and Solomon. The kingdom in the time of Isaiah was in decline, long since divided into a southern kingdom of 'Judah' and a northern kingdom of 'Ephraim'.[46] The northern kingdom fell to the Assyrians during Isaiah's lifetime. The conquest of Judah, the southern kingdom where Isaiah lived, loomed on the horizon.

Who was the prophet Isaiah? In ancient Jewish Holy Scriptures not only his own book attests to his historical presence but also 2 Kings and 2 Chronicles attest to his existence. Isaiah was born the son of Amoz about 760 years before Jesus. Isaiah's role as an official to Judah's King Uzziah indicates he was probably of a privileged family in Jerusalem. Rabbinic tradition says he was a cousin of King Uzziah. Chapter 6 of the book of Isaiah recorded his spectacular vision of God in the Temple, an aftermath of King Uzziah's death in 740 BC. The distraught Isaiah found comfort in his vision of the everlasting King. This began his calling as a prophet.

Isaiah named his two sons Maher-Shalal-Hash-Baz (Hebrew for 'Speed-the-Spoil/Hasten-the-Booty') and Shear-Jashub (Hebrew for 'A-Remnant-Shall-Return'). These names reflected the two themes of the book of Isaiah. First, warned Isaiah, the Jews of Judah would be severely punished by God and sent into exile. Then a remnant would return. Within these broad themes were many Messianic prophecies. One of the more prominent ones prophesied that although the tree of the House of David would fall, a stump would remain. Out of that stump would sprout the eventual Messiah.

After King Uzziah's death, Jotham reigned for 18 years, then Ahaz for 19 years, then Hezekiah for 29 years. Isaiah's influence on royalty peaked under devout King Hezekiah. As God's instrument Isaiah helped Hezekiah turn away an attack by the Assyrians in 701 BC. Nevertheless, Isaiah's warnings did not prevent Judah's disintegration. Rabbinic tradition says Hezekiah's evil successor, King Manasseh, martyred Isaiah—although by that time Isaiah was nearly 90 years old.

For his own Holy Scripture Isaiah certainly read the five books of the Pentateuch and the books of the former prophets Joshua, Judges, Samuel and 1 Kings. Also he must have read in some form the books of Psalms and Proverbs. The only books of latter prophets that Isaiah might have known were those of Jonah and Amos—and possibly those of his contemporaries, Hosea and Micah. He certainly did not know the books of prophets that came after him: Ezekiel, Daniel, Nahum, Zepahaniah, Habakkuk, Jeremiah, Obadiah, Zechariah, Haggai and Malachi.

Isaiah wrote both prose and poetry. His poetry is superb, extremely rich in imagery. His purpose could be sweet in tone, as in Isaiah 66:12–13:

> For this is what the Lord says:
> "I will extend peace to her like a river, and the wealth of nations like a flooding stream; you will nurse and be carried on her arm and dandled on her knees.
> As a mother comforts her child, so will I comfort you; and you will be comforted over Jerusalem."

Or his purpose could be severe, as in Isaiah 30:27–28:

> See, the Name of the Lord comes from afar, with burning anger and dense clouds of smoke; his lips are full of wrath, and his tongue is a consuming fire.
> His breath is like a rushing torrent, rising up to the neck.
> He shakes the nations in the sieve of destruction; he places in the jaws of the peoples a bit that leads them astray.

The first 39 chapters of the 66-chapter book of Isaiah warn of God's approaching judgment on the Jews, God's chosen but sinful people. The first major theme is Isaiah's prophecies against the Jews. It spans the first 12 chapters. The warning is not one long strident harangue. Interspersed with dire warnings are prophecies of comfort that their decline would not be everlasting. In spite of the Jews' iniquities, days of glory are also ahead. Early in his book Isaiah promised triumph (Isaiah 2:2-3):

> In the last days the mountain of the Lord's temple will be established as chief among the mountains; it will be raised above the hills, and all nations will stream to it.
> Many peoples will come and say,
>> "Come, let us go up to the mountain of the Lord, to the house of the God of Jacob.
>> He will teach us his ways, so that we may walk in his paths."
> The law will go out from Zion, the word of the Lord from Jerusalem.

Isaiah provided much comfort by his visions of the future Messiah—a descendant of David. In Isaiah 9:6 he revealed that Galilee would be honored, 'For to us a child is born', 'Wonderful Counselor, Mighty God, Everlasting Father, Prince of Peace...'. In chapters 11 and 12 he reinforced his promise of the Messiah and a future kingdom of total peace. 'The wolf will live with the lamb', prophesied Isaiah 11:6. 'A shoot will come up from the root of Jesse', promised Isaiah 11:10.

Chapters 13 through 23 contain prophecies against nations known to Isaiah. None of the neighbors would be spared. Babylonians, Assyrians, Philistines and Egyptians were all doomed. Jerusalem was included as well. Chapters 24 through 27 dealt with the end time. God's final judgment would 'lay waste' to the earth. Although chapter 27 contained God's promise that a remnant of the Jews would be restored, chapters 28 through 34 were a litany of woes for the Jews. Still, even in those troubled passages Isaiah offered glimpses of Messianic hope for the future in 'a precious cornerstone' (28:16). And what could be more comforting than 'your covenant with death will be annulled' (28:18)? Finally in Isaiah 35:4 he announced that God 'will come to save you'.

Chapters 36 through 39 jolt readers of today in that the story abruptly becomes historical. Suddenly Isaiah introduced King Hezekiah. Assyrians besieged Hezekiah's Jerusalem. Isaiah was personally involved in these historical events. With Isaiah's counsel Hezekiah managed to save Jerusalem. But in chapter 39 Isaiah predicted to Hezekiah himself that the Jews would eventually be carried off into Babylon. That disaster occurred 100 years later.

Just as the first 39 chapters of the book of Isaiah are predominantly woeful, the last 27 chapters are predominantly comforting. Yes, comfort abruptly follows Isaiah's terrifying prediction about exile of all Jews into Babylon. Few verses expressed the theme better than Isaiah 40:1-2:

> Comfort, comfort my people, says your God.
> Speak tenderly to Jerusalem, and proclaim to her that her hard service has been completed, that her sin has been paid for, that she has received from the Lord's hand double for all her sins.

Isaiah demonstrates this theme of suffering by God's chosen people with his very dramatic depiction of the 'Suffering Servant'. Although the Psalms preceded Isaiah with glimpses of the Messiah as a much-suffering servant, Isaiah develops the concept fully. This concept offended many Jews. Was the Messiah not going to be a great warrior-king like David? Perhaps, some explained, Isaiah's Suffering Servant did not represent the Messiah but represented the nation of Israel. In Isaiah 41:8, God says very pointedly, "But you, Oh Israel, my servant..." Christians need not be disturbed by this. This is an example of a Bible prophecy that not only had a second meaning, but a greater meaning. The Servant's suffering, death and redemption of mankind were no less than prophecies of the Messiah fulfilled by Jesus.

Isaiah composed what later became known as the four 'Servant Songs'. The first is Isaiah 42:1-9. God introduces him, "Here is my servant, whom I uphold, my chosen one in whom I delight..." This song also says the servant would be "a light for the Gentiles". The second 'Servant Song', Isaiah 49:1-13, includes "you may bring my salvation to the ends of the earth". The third song, Isaiah 50:4-11, increases the theme that the servant would be persecuted. The suffering of the Servant reaches a crescendo in the fourth song: Isaiah 52:13 to 53:12. Virtually every detailed line of that song was fulfilled by Jesus, including the stunning prophecy of his resurrection in Isaiah 53:11: "After the suffering of his soul, he will see the light of life"![47]

Chapters 60 through 66 concluded the book of Isaiah with glories of the future age. The coming of the Messiah in Chapter 61 was the highlight. But in addition to the promised Redeemer the main themes were that long life and peace await the faithful, and everlasting torment await the unfaithful.[48]

Now see how Jesus and his followers loved the great book of Isaiah...

< 13 >

HOW JESUS LOVED ISAIAH

And how well did Jesus love Isaiah?

Jesus appealed to Isaiah eight times, nearly 20 percent of his quotes of Jewish Holy Scriptures. He drew equally from the first part (on judgment) of Isaiah and the second part (on comfort). He quoted each part four times. It is obvious that he lived and breathed the book of Isaiah, just as he fulfilled Isaiah's prophecies. He made use of Isaiah in all situations: to hostile Jewish authorities, to sympathetic crowds, and to his disciples. Often by quoting Isaiah he revealed he was the Messiah or that terrible times were ahead. Of course those revelations shocked his listeners.

Jesus used an abbreviated version of Isaiah 6:9-10 in speaking to his disciples in Mark 4:11-12:

> He told them, "The secret of the kingdom of God has been given to you. But to those on the outside everything is said in parables so that,
> 'they may be ever seeing but never perceiving, and ever hearing but never understanding; otherwise they might turn and be forgiven!'"

Yes, in the book of Isaiah God had previously referred to certain hard-hearted people of Israel. 'For how long?' Isaiah had asked God. Until utter catastrophe, replied God. Cities would be destroyed. All but a remnant of the Jews would disappear. And all that prophecy was fulfilled by the invasion of Babylon and the exile of the Jews. Did the disciples of Jesus perceive from this particular quotation from Isaiah a catastrophe of like proportions in their own future?

When Jesus spoke to Peter, James, John and Andrew on the Mount of Olives he combined Isaiah 13:10 verbatim with a looser rendition of Isaiah 34:4, as recorded in Mark 13:24-26:

> But in those days, following that distress, 'the sun will be dark-
> ened, and the moon will not give its light; the stars will fall
> from the sky, and the heavenly bodies will be shaken.'
> At that time men will see the Son of Man coming in clouds with
> great power and glory...

The quotes of these passages of Isaiah are both unique to Jesus in the New Testament. Isaiah 13:10 prophesied days of wrath against Baby-lon. However Isaiah 34:4 foretold God's judgment against all the na-tions. Jesus adroitly employed the imageries of widely separated passages of Isaiah to describe another time of wrath. Did disciples of Jesus recognize from this particular quotation a catastrophe of like proportions in their own future? Certainly. However Jesus lightened that depressing warning about terrible times ahead with the promise of his return — his 'second coming'. Note however that he later stated no one knows when he will return again (Mark 13:32). Not the angels. Not even Jesus. Only the Father.

Jesus cited Isaiah 29:13 to the teachers of the Law in Mark 7:6-9:

> He replied, "Isaiah was right when he prophesied about you
> hypocrites; as it is written:
> 'These people honor me with their lips, but their hearts are far
> from me.
> They worship me in vain; their teachings are but rules taught
> by men.'
> You have let go of the commands of God and are holding on to
> the traditions of men."

Teachers of the Law had confronted Jesus over his disciples eating with 'unclean hands'. Jewish religious leaders sent to observe his min-istry in Galilee focused on violations of trivial 'laws' that they them-selves had created. That angered Jesus. That was legalism carried to the point of oppression, as well as being hypocritical. Isaiah 29:13 was the exact sentiment against the same kind of hypocrisy over 700 years before.

Now consider quotations from the second part of Isaiah, that part characterized by Isaiah's message of comfort. Jesus made use of Isaiah 54:13 while speaking to a crowd of believers and skeptics, as recorded in John 6:45:

> It is written in the Prophets: 'They will all be taught by God.'

This verse from Isaiah 54:13 was God's promise to the Jews of the future glory of Zion. But Jesus directed the passage at certain followers who were grumbling about his hints of being divine. People were not drawn to him, explained Jesus, unless God compelled them to follow him. All who listened to the Father and learned from him came to Jesus for salvation. For Jesus had preceded his quote of Isaiah with the shocking assertion that anyone who came to him would be raised by him on the last day!

Jesus recited Isaiah 56:7 to a crowd at the Temple in Jerusalem after driving out the merchants. Mark 11:17 recorded him saying:

> Is it not written: 'My house will be called a house of prayer for all nations'?

Jesus followed this passage with another passage (from Jeremiah), 'But you have made it a den of robbers,' referring to the money changers and to those selling animals for sacrifice. Here Jesus used Isaiah 56:7 in a much narrower sense than the original meaning. For the original pronouncement by God was a prophetic invitation to all the nations — Gentiles as well as Jews — in the glory of Zion. But Jesus also wanted his listeners to reflect on the contrast: Isaiah's future glory of Zion compared to the tawdry spectacle of the Temple under King Herod.

That Isaiah 61:1–2 was intentionally selected and read by Jesus in the synagogue at Nazareth was recorded in Luke 4:17–19:

> The scroll of the prophet Isaiah was handed to him. Unrolling it, he found the place where it is written:
> The Spirit of the Lord is on me, because he has anointed me to preach good news to the poor.
> He has sent me to proclaim freedom for the prisoners and recovery of sight for the blind, to release the oppressed, to proclaim the year of the Lord's favor.

Then Jesus added those shocking words, "Today this scripture is fulfilled in your hearing," to open the ministry of the Messiah. For this passage of Isaiah definitely prophesied the Messiah. And it set the tone for the last section in Isaiah that promised future glory.

In Mark 9:47–48 Jesus drew upon Isaiah 66:24 while speaking privately to his disciples:

> And if your eye causes you to sin, pluck it out. It is better for you to enter the kingdom of God with one eye than to have two eyes and be thrown into hell, where 'their worm does not die, and the fire is not quenched.'

Stop sinning, Jesus warned, no matter what the cost. Hellfire was going to be far worse. And hellfire is the fate of all who rebel against God. Of course at that point Jesus had not yet atoned for the sins of mankind. Nor had he said that he would. His message urged people to prepare for the kingdom of God. Isaiah's purpose was exactly the same. Yes, when the end came God would judge and give mercy. But those who had rebelled against God faced terrible punishment.

In summary Jesus quoted Isaiah in many situations. He knew it so well he could deftly combine widely separated passages to make a point. He drew on Isaiah to speak of end times, both turmoil and glory. He employed Isaiah against hypocrites. He often used Isaiah in a Messianic sense. In Nazareth he certainly drew upon Isaiah in one dramatic situation to emphasize that he was the Messiah. The most puzzling aspect about his usage is that he never once quoted any of the four Servant Songs, those very graphic prophecies of Jesus himself.

Now discover how well his followers loved Isaiah...

< 14 >

HOW PAUL LOVED ISAIAH

How well did Paul love Isaiah?

Paul quoted Isaiah 28 times, over one-fourth of his total quotes from the Jewish Scriptures. All but one of Paul's quotations of Isaiah occurs in Acts or in his letters to the Romans and the Corinthians. Consider his uses of Isaiah in the order that they appear in the New Testament].

The first occurrence was recorded by Luke in Acts 13:34. Paul recited Isaiah 55:3:

> The fact that God raised him from the dead, never to decay, is stated in these words: 'I will give you the holy and sure blessings promised to David.'

Paul had brought the good news of the resurrection to Jews and Gentiles at Antioch in Pisidia. On this occasion he spoke at the synagogue. He quoted several Old Testament passages in succession to explain how the Messiah and salvation of mankind had been promised by God in the past.

Acts 13 also tells us Paul and Barnabas returned to that same synagogue the next Sabbath. This time the Jews were angry. Why were the two missionaries delivering the Gospel to Gentiles? Paul and Barnabas explained that they had felt obligated to deliver the Gospel to the Jews first. But now that the Jews had rejected it they would turn to the Gentiles. Then the two missionaries justified their actions by drawing upon part of the second Servant Song (Isaiah 49:6) in Acts 13:47:

> For this is what the Lord has commanded us: 'I have made you a light for the Gentiles, that you may bring salvation to the ends of the earth.'

When Paul first arrived in Rome to await trial he spoke all day to a large group of Jews. He convinced some that Jesus fulfilled the prophecies. But many he could not convince. In exasperation Paul recited the complete passage of Isaiah 6:9–10 (recorded by Luke in Acts 28:25–27):

> "The Holy Spirit spoke the truth to your forefathers when he said through Isaiah the prophet:
>> 'Go to this people and say, "You will be ever hearing but never understanding; you will be ever seeing but never perceiving."
> For this people's heart has become calloused; they hardly hear with their ears, and they have closed their eyes.
> Otherwise they might see with their eyes, hear with their ears, understand with their hearts and turn, and I would heal them."

It had been a long day after many years of effort with his fellow Jews and Paul was frustrated. After this condemnation of most of his Jewish listeners Paul warned them that the Gentiles eagerly listened to his message of the Jewish Messiah!

Now consider how Paul quoted Isaiah in his letter to the Romans. He used no less than 16 quotes from Isaiah. Paul invoked Isaiah 52:5 in Romans 2:24 to chide the Jews about the way they abused the 'Law':

> As it is written: "God's name is blasphemed among the Gentiles because of you."

Isaiah and Paul differed in their use here. Isaiah prophesied the Babylonians would mock their captive Israelites by blaspheming God. But Paul believed Jews of his day caused Gentiles to blaspheme God because the Gentiles could see the Jews were hypocrites about their own laws.

> Paul recalled Isaiah 59:7–8 in Romans 3:15–17:
> "Their feet are swift to shed blood; ruin and misery mark their ways, and the way of peace they do not know."

Isaiah condemned sinful Israelites. For Paul this was but one quote in a sequence of Old Testament quotes he used to prove no one was righteous in the 'Law' or in any other way except through faith in Christ.

> Paul drew on Isaiah 29:16 in his letter to the Romans (9:20):

> "Shall what is formed say to him who formed it, 'Why did you make me like this?'"

Isaiah pointed out the absurdity of the created questioning the Creator. Isaiah believed God had the 'unquestionable' sovereign right to reject Israel. This quote was in the section of Paul's letter that defended what he too considered God's sovereign right to reject Israel.

Isaiah 10:22–23 served Paul in Romans 9:27–28:

> Isaiah cries out concerning Israel:
> "Though the number of the Israelites be like the sand by the sea, only the remnant will be saved.
> For the Lord will carry out his sentence on earth with speed and finality."

Isaiah was preparing the Jews of his time for the harsh exile ahead when only a remnant would return to Israel. It was only through God's grace that a remnant of Jews would survive. Paul used this quote to illustrate again God's sovereignty.

Paul then went on to apply Isaiah 1:9 in Romans 9:29:

> It is just as Isaiah said previously:
> "Unless the Lord Almighty had left us descendants, we would have become like Sodom, we would have been like Gomorrah."

Yes, it was only through God's grace that the Jewish descendants did not perish like all the sinners at Sodom and Gomorrah.

In Romans 9:33 Paul combined portions of Isaiah 28:16, 8:14 and 28:16 a second time to read:

> As it is written:
> "See, I lay in Zion a stone that causes men to stumble and a rock that makes them fall, and the one who trusts in him will never be put to shame."

Paul did not refer here to Jesus but to faith. He claimed the Israelites — God's chosen people — had pursued righteousness not by faith but by good works.

Isaiah 52: 7 helped Paul justify his missionary calling (in Romans 10:15):

> And how can they preach unless they are sent? As it is written, "How beautiful are the feet of those who bring good news!"

Of course Paul referred to the good news, the 'Gospel', of Jesus and of salvation that the followers of Jesus brought. Isaiah referred to the future news brought by messengers that the exiles were returning.

Paul's quote of Isaiah 53:1 in Romans 10:16 was from Isaiah's fourth Servant Song. This Servant Song epitomized the Servant's suffering. Jesus fulfilled virtually every detailed line of that song of persecution and execution. Paul and the followers of Jesus made use of the fourth Servant Song no fewer than eight times. For that reason the entire song is quoted in the next chapter. Note that in Romans 10:16 Paul's purpose for using Isaiah 53:1, "Lord, who has believed our message?", was essentially the same as Isaiah's original purpose: many would not believe.

Isaiah 65:1-2 Paul cited in Romans 10:20-21:

> And Isaiah boldly says,
>> "I was found by those who did not seek me; I revealed myself to those who did not ask for me.
> But concerning Israel he says,
>> "All day long I have held out my hands to a disobedient and obstinate people."

Both Isaiah and Paul used this to emphasize how Gentiles accepted God's truth but the Jews stubbornly resisted God's truth.

Isaiah 29:10 Paul recalled in Romans 11:8:

> as it is written:
>> "God gave them a spirit of stupor, eyes so that they could not see and ears so that they could not hear, to this very day."

Paul quoted this passage – similar sounding to Isaiah 6:9-10 but quite different in purpose – to emphasize that by grace God chose a remnant of the Jews to be the 'elect'. All others were in a stupor.

Isaiah 59:20-21 helped Paul in Romans 11:26-27:

> And so all Israel will be saved, as it is written:
>> "The deliverer will come from Zion; he will turn godlessness away from Jacob.
>> And this is my covenant with them when I take away their sins."

Isaiah was expounding on the glory of Zion. But Paul quoted Isaiah to show that although Paul enlisted Gentiles he knew all Israel would be saved eventually too. So Gentiles must not be conceited.

Isaiah 40:13 served Paul in Romans 11:34:

> "For who has known the mind of the Lord that he may instruct him?"

Paul invoked this quote from Isaiah in awe of God's unfathomable riches. Paul used this quote a second time, in 1 Corinthians 2:16 There the intent of both Isaiah and Paul was obvious: Who can question the will of God? Paul was still developing the point that scholars and philosophers considered all talk of God foolishness.

Portions of Isaiah 45:23 Paul employed in his letter to the Romans (14:11):

> It is written:
> "'As surely as I live,' says the Lord, 'every knee will bow before me; every tongue will confess to God.'"

Paul used this passage from Isaiah to chastise believers for judging their brothers. Each one would give his own account to God soon enough, he noted after the quote.

Paul made use of Isaiah 11:10 in Romans 15:12:

> And again, Isaiah says,
> "The Root of Jesse will spring up, one who will arise to rule over the nations; the Gentiles will hope in him."

Paul employed this Messianic prophecy of Isaiah to convince the Romans that Jesus was not only a 'servant of the Jews' but the Gentiles.

Paul's quote of Isaiah 52:15 in Romans 15:21 was from Isaiah's fourth Servant Song:

> Rather, as it is written:
> "Those who were not told about him will see, and those who have not heard will understand."

Because it was one of Isaiah's very strong Messianic prophecies Paul used it in the same sense. It justified his life mission of spreading the Gospel.

Next use by Paul of Isaiah was in his letters to the Corinthians. Paul cited Isaiah 29:14 in 1 Corinthians 1:19:

> For it is written:
> "I will destroy the wisdom of the wise; the intelligence of the intelligent I will frustrate."

Isaiah referred to the people of Jerusalem. God would confound the unbelievers. In the context of this passage from Isaiah Paul explained that Christ sent him to preach the Gospel, not by words of wisdom but by the message of the cross. The unbelievers would deem the message foolish; the believers would be empowered by God.

Paul applied Isaiah 64:4 in 1 Corinthians 2:9:

> However, as it is written:
> "No eye has seen, no ear has heard, no mind has conceived what God has prepared for those who love him"

Isaiah was expounding on the glory that awaited Zion. As mentioned before, Paul was developing in 1 Corinthians a point that the scholar, the wise man and the philosopher all consider talk of God foolishness. But the Christians were destined to have secret wisdom from God.

Paul worked Isaiah 28:11-12 into 1 Corinthians 14:21:

> ...it is written:
> "Through men of strange tongues and through the lips of foreigners I will speak to this people, but even then they will not listen to me," says the Lord.

Isaiah was dealing with Israel's ignorance that God had made the nation a wonderful resting place for the faithful, even placing a 'precious cornerstone' there for salvation. Paul used it as a prophecy of 'speaking in tongues', a gift of the Holy Spirit widely used by followers of Jesus at the Pentecost and many believers thereafter.

Also in Paul's first letter to the Corinthians he made use of Isaiah 22:13 (1 Corinthians 15:32):

> If the dead are not raised, "Let us eat and drink, for tomorrow we die."

Both Paul and Isaiah employed it for the same purpose. It was contrary to God's wishes and it was jolting. It was nothing less than the Epicurean belief, a philosophy without hope, that originated in Greece many hundreds of years after Isaiah.

Isaiah 25:08 Paul quoted in the same chapter of his letter to the Corinthians (1 Corinthians 15:54):

> When the perishable has been clothed with the imperishable, and the mortal with immortality, then the saying that is written will come true: "Death has been swallowed up in victory."

For both Isaiah and Paul this was Messianic prophecy. This was what Isaiah and Paul really believed – in contrast to the previous 'eat and drink, for tomorrow we die' passage.

In Paul's second letter to the Corinthians he used Isaiah 49:8 (in 2 Corinthians 6:1–2):

> As God's fellow workers we urge you not to receive God's grace in vain. For he says,
> "In the time of my favor I heard you, and in the day of salvation I helped you."
> I tell you, now is the time of God's favor, now is the day of salvation.

Paul's purpose in recalling part of Isaiah's second Servant Song was clear. He urged righteousness among the believers at Corinth. God had blessed the believers. They must not fail God.

In the same letter Paul cited part of Isaiah 52:11 in 2 Corinthians 6:17:

> "Therefore come out from them and be separate, says the Lord. Touch no unclean thing, and I will receive you."

Isaiah warned his Israelites to leave Babylon with themselves as pure as possible. Paul employed the passage in his plea to Christians to live righteously. They had to avoid unbelievers. Remain separate, he warned.

The last occurrence of Paul making use of Isaiah was most likely in his letter to the Galatians. He quoted Isaiah 54:1 in Galatians 4:27:

> For it is written:
> "Be glad, O barren woman, who bears no children; break forth and cry aloud, you who have no labor pains; because more are the children of the desolate woman than of her who has a husband."

Isaiah used these verses of a barren woman—like Abraham's barren Sarah—as a metaphor for the Jerusalem that was going to be barren during the exile, yet eventually prolific. In Galatians, Paul used Isaiah's metaphor to emphasize the young Christian church was the same as Abraham's 'children of promise'.

In summary, the New Testament recorded that in Acts and in his letters Paul quoted Isaiah to diverse audiences for many purposes. But certainly the main use of Isaiah was to confirm Jesus was the Messiah prophesied by Isaiah. Often Paul quoted Isaiah to reassure Gentiles too. Regarding use of the first part of Isaiah (on judgment) relative to the second part (on comfort), Paul favored the second part 16 to 12.

How did the other followers love Isaiah? Consider that next...

< 15 >

HOW OTHER FOLLOWERS OF JESUS LOVED ISAIAH

Note again: this chapter details how the followers of Jesus — *other than Paul* — loved Isaiah. How well did the other followers of Jesus love Isaiah? They quoted Isaiah 20 times in their Gospel narratives, Acts and letters. Isaiah accounts for over 20 percent of all their quotations of the Old Testament. Chapter 13 reviews the quotations of Isaiah by Jesus by their sequence within Isaiah. Chapter 14 however reviews Paul's quotes of Isaiah in the order that they appear in the New Testament. Now, this chapter on the quotations of Isaiah by the followers of Jesus will revert to their sequence within Isaiah. So first consider chapters 1 through 39 of Isaiah, that part dubbed by some scholars the 'book of judgment'.

Like Jesus, John 12:40–41 drew upon Isaiah 6:9–10 as appropriate for the hard-hearted people of Israel. But Isaiah 7:14 was quoted only in Matthew 1:23:

> All this took place to fulfill what the Lord had said through the prophet: "The virgin will be with child and will give birth to a son, and they will call him Immanuel" — which means, 'God with us.'

Obviously Matthew used this passage from Isaiah to verify the prophecy of the Messiah's virgin birth. One might ask why Luke, the apostle who so clearly recorded recollections of Mary about the virgin birth, did not cite this passage too.

The followers of Jesus quoted chapter 8 of Isaiah three times. A portion of Isaiah 8:14 was cited in 1 Peter 2:8. Peter wrote that, for unbelievers, Christ was:

> A stone that causes men to stumble and a rock that makes them fall.

The second half of Isaiah 8:12 Peter used in 1 Peter 3:14:

> But even if you should suffer for what is right, you are blessed. "Do not fear what they fear..."

Peter was obviously encouraging the believers with these passages from Isaiah.

Portions of Isaiah 8:17–18 are portrayed in Hebrews 2:13 as the very words of Jesus:

> "I will put my trust in him." And again he says, "Here am I, and the children God has given me."

Jesus put his trust completely in God who gave him mankind as his brothers and children. So Jesus could share in humanity.

Isaiah 9:1–2, which prophesied the Messiah would arise in Galilee, Matthew made use of loosely (in Matthew 4:15–16):

> Land of Zebulun and land of Naphtali, the way to the sea, along the Jordan, Galilee of the Gentiles — the people living in darkness have seen a great light; on those living in the land of the shadow of death a light has dawned.

The reason for the quote Matthew had prefaced in 4:13–14: 'Leaving Nazareth, he (Jesus) went and lived in Capernaum, which was by the lake in the area of Zebulun and Naphtali—to fulfill what was said through the prophet Isaiah'.

The Messianic message of Isaiah 28:16 Peter applied in 1 Peter 2:6:

> For in Scripture it says:
> "See, I lay a stone in Zion, a chosen and precious cornerstone, and the one who trusts in him will never be put to shame."

The meaning of this metaphor of the cornerstone for the followers of Jesus was obvious.

Now consider the second part of Isaiah, that part termed by some scholars the 'book of comfort'. One passage — Isaiah 40:3–8 — was collectively quoted in its entirety: John 1:23 and Mark 1:3 called upon Isaiah 40:3; Luke 3:4–6 cited Isaiah 40:3–5 ; and 1 Peter 1:24–25 used Isaiah 40:6–8. In its entirety Isaiah 40:3–8 said:

> A voice of one calling:
> "In the desert prepare the way for the Lord; make straight in the wilderness a highway for our God.

> Every valley shall be raised up, every mountain and hill made low; the rough ground shall become level, the rugged places a plain.
> And the glory of the Lord will be revealed, and all mankind together will see it. For the mouth of the Lord has spoken."
> A voice says, "Cry out." And I said, "What shall I cry?"
> "All men are like grass, and all their glory is like the flowers of the field.
> The grass withers and the flowers fall, because the breath of the Lord blows on them. Surely the people are grass.
> The grass withers and the flowers fall, but the word of our God stands forever."

All followers of Jesus realized this prophecy by Isaiah about one in the desert preparing the way for the lord was fulfilled by John the Baptist (whom Jesus called the 'greatest of men').

Verses 1 through 4 of the first of the four Servant Songs (Isaiah 42:1–9) Matthew used in his narrative (Matthew 12:18–21):

> 'Here is my servant whom I have chosen, the one I love, in whom I delight;
> I will put my Spirit on him, and he will proclaim justice to the nations.
> He will not quarrel or cry out; no one will hear his voice in the streets.
> A bruised reed he will not break, and a smoldering wick he will not snuff out, till he leads justice to victory.
> In his name the nations will put their hope.'

Of course Matthew was applying Isaiah to Jesus. At this time Jesus was urging people he had healed not to broadcast his miracles.

From the first Servant Song Luke 2:29–32 included one phrase of Isaiah 42:7 – 'a light for revelation to the Gentiles'.

The speaker was Simeon, a righteous man in Jerusalem, who believed he would not die before he saw the Messiah. The Holy Spirit drew him to the Temple where he saw the infant Jesus being consecrated to God after 40 days of purification.

The followers of Jesus knew first-hand the prophecy of Isaiah's fourth Servant Song (Isaiah 52:13–53:12). They quoted portions of the Song no fewer than six times (Paul had also quoted it twice). For that reason the entire song follows here:

See, my servant will act wisely; he will be raised and lifted up and highly exalted.

Just as there were many who were appalled at him—his appearance was so disfigured beyond that of any man and his form marred beyond human likeness—so will he sprinkle many nations, and kings will shut their mouths because of him.

For what they were not told, they will see, and what they have not heard, they will understand.

Who has believed our message and to whom has the arm of the Lord been revealed?

He grew up before him like a tender shoot, and like a root out of dry ground.

He had no beauty or majesty to attract us to him, nothing in his appearance that we should desire him.

He was despised and rejected by men, a man of sorrows, and familiar with suffering.

Like one from whom men hide their faces he was despised, and we esteemed him not.

Surely he took up our infirmities and carried our sorrows, yet we considered him stricken by God, smitten by him, and afflicted.

But he was pierced for our transgressions, he was crushed for our iniquities; the punishment that brought us peace was upon him, and by his wounds we are healed.

We all, like sheep, have gone astray, each of us has turned to his own way; and the Lord has laid on him the iniquity of us all.

He was oppressed and afflicted, yet he did not open his mouth; he was led like a lamb to the slaughter, and as a sheep before her shearers is silent, so he did not open his mouth.

By oppression and judgment he was taken away. And who can speak of his descendants?

For he was cut off from the land of the living; for the transgression of my people he was stricken.

He was assigned a grave with the wicked, and with the rich in his death, though he had done no violence, nor was any deceit in his mouth.

Yet it was the Lord's will to crush him and cause him to suffer, and though the Lord makes his life a guilt offering, he will see his offspring and prolong his days, and the will of the Lord will prosper in his hand.

> After the suffering of his soul, he will see the light and be satis-
> fied; by his knowledge my righteous servant will justify
> many, and he will bear their iniquities.
> Therefore I will give him a portion among the great, and he will
> divide the spoils with the strong, because he poured out his
> life unto death, and was numbered with the transgressors.
> For he bore the sin of many, and made intercession for the
> transgressors.

In succession, the Fourth Servant Song (Isaiah 52:13–53:12) was quoted in John 12:38 (Isaiah 53:1), Matthew 8:7 (Isaiah 53:4), 1 Peter 2:24–25 (Isaiah 53:5–6), Acts 8:32–33 (Isaiah 53:7–8), 1 Peter 2:22 (Isaiah 53:9), and Mark 15:28 (Isaiah 53:12). Isaiah 53:12 occurred only in some manuscripts of Mark, in which 15:28 reads: "They crucified two robbers with him, one on his right and one on his left, and the scripture was fulfilled which says. ' He was counted with the lawless ones.'"

God's mighty words in Isaiah 66:1–2 were recited by Stephen in Acts 7:49–50:

> 'Heaven is my throne, and the earth is my footstool.
> What kind of house will you build for me? says the Lord. Or
> where will my resting place be?
> Has not my hand made all these things?'

This passage from Isaiah carried much heat with it, for what followed it in Isaiah was not only God's condemnation of the Jewish sacrifices but his preference for 'he who is humble and contrite, and trembles at my word'. Stephen also followed the quote with his own harsh words — unfortunately, his last.

In summary, the followers of Jesus (other than Paul) quoted Isaiah to diverse audiences. Certainly their main purpose was to confirm Jesus as the prophesied Messiah. They favored the second part (on comfort) to the first part (on judgment) by a count of 13 to 7.

Of the 56 total quotations of Isaiah in the New Testament, Jesus and his followers favored the part on comfort 34 to 23, possibly a significant preference.[49] The 10 chapters from 30 to 39 they almost ignored. Those chapters included woes on Egypt and Assyria as well as the historical record of the Assyrian siege on Jerusalem. Only Jesus quoted from these shunned chapters, on one occasion to prophesy God's wrath against the nations in the end time.

Next consider how Jesus and his followers loved the 'Twelve'...

< 16 >

HOW JESUS AND HIS FOLLOWERS LOVED THE 'TWELVE'

Recall that for Jesus and his followers all the prophets occur in two groups. One of these groups includes Joshua, Judges, Samuel and Kings. Readers of today call this group the 'historical books', but ancient Jews called this group the 'former prophets'. The ancient Jews recognized a second group of prophets — which they called the 'latter prophets'. The latter prophets include Isaiah, Jeremiah and Ezekiel. Today's readers call these three the 'major prophets' and include Daniel as well. The ancient Jews included Daniel in the 'Writings'.

Also included in the 'latter prophets' of the ancient Jews is the assemblage of prophets called today the 'minor prophets'. They are 'minor' to readers of today only in the sense that their books are short in length. In the time of Jesus they were called collectively the 'Twelve' because all were usually scribed on one scroll. The Twelve were probably arranged in three subgroups of contemporaries. Many scholars believe Hosea, Joel, Amos, Obadiah, Jonah and Micah all prophesied during the times of Assyrian power (roughly 800–700 BC).[50] Nahum, Habakkuk and Zephaniah were prominent during the decline of Assyria (about 700–600 BC). Haggai, Zechariah and Malachi prophesied after the Jews returned from captivity (the 'exile') in Babylon around 550 BC. This order of books for the 'Twelve' was maintained in the Old Testament of the Christian Bible.

Consider the 'Twelve' below however in the order of their 'popularity' for use. First among the Twelve is the book of Hosea, from which seven quotations were drawn for use in the New Testament. Hosea is a peculiar book. At its beginning (Hosea 1:2), God gave Hosea an astonishing command:

> "Go, take to yourself an adulterous wife and children of unfaithfulness, because the land is guilty of the vilest adultery in departing from the Lord."

So Hosea married Gomer. Many scholars debate whether Hosea's marriage to Gomer is real or a literary device. Is the marriage a metaphor for God's faithfulness to unfaithful Israel? That seems the overriding theme in the book of Hosea.

Jesus and his followers used wonderful quotations from the book of Hosea. Jesus used Hosea 6:6 — "I desire mercy, not sacrifice" — twice in Matthew. In Matthew 9:13 Jesus quotes these words of God to answer Pharisees who question his association with sinners. In the same verse Jesus adds 'I have not come to call the righteous, but sinners'. Implied also is the rest of the scripture from Hosea: 'acknowledge God rather than burn offerings'.[51] Jesus employed the same quotation from Hosea in Matthew 12:7, again in a confrontation with the Pharisees over a legalism.

Jesus recalled Hosea 10:08 in Luke 23:30:

> Then 'they will say to the mountains, "Fall on us!" and to the hills, "Cover us!"'

In Hosea God announced that dreadful days of punishment lay ahead for the sinners of Israel. These chilling words Jesus recited to his women followers on his way to be crucified. Terrible times were ahead for the Jews.

Hosea 11:1 was used in the narration of Matthew 2:15:

> And so was fulfilled what the Lord had said through the prophet: "Out of Egypt I called my son."

Hosea referred to the exodus led by Moses. But Matthew recognized a second meaning. As noted above, Joseph and Mary fled with the infant Jesus to Egypt to escape the murderous King Herod. After Herod died, the refugees were able to leave Egypt, thus fulfilling another prophecy.

Hebrews 13:15 made use of a ringing phrase of Hosea 14:2:

> Through Jesus, therefore, let us continually offer to God a sacrifice of praise — the fruit of lips that confess his name.

Hosea 14:2 urged Jews to say to God: "Forgive all our sins and receive us graciously, that we may offer the fruit of our lips." In other words, God wanted words of repentance, not animal or grain sacrifice.

In Romans 9:25–26 Paul combined quotes of Hosea 2:23, then Hosea 1:10:

> As he says in Hosea:
> "I will call them 'my people' who are not my people; and I will call her 'my loved one' who is not my loved one,"
> and, "It will happen that in the very place where it was said to them, 'You are not my people,' they will be called 'sons of the living God.'"

Hosea referred to the Israelites themselves after reconciliation with God. But as he did so often, Paul applied Jewish Scriptures to assure Gentiles it had been prophesied that some of them would indeed be 'children of God'.

Paul recalled Hosea 13:14 in 1 Corinthians 15:55:

> "Where, O death, is your victory? Where, O death, is your sting?"

Hosea used these words as a metaphor for the death of Israel. Paul used it for a second meaning: believers in Christ would be resurrected. Paul's resounding note of encouragement was immediately preceded by an allusion to Isaiah 25:8.[52]

The prophet Habakkuk lived almost long enough to see the exile. He agonized over the unfairness of life. Why did the righteous suffer so? Why weren't the wicked punished? The New Testament writers quoted Habakkuk's tiny book probably more often per word of scripture than any other book in the Old Testament. Barely 1000 words, the book of Habakkuk was quoted four times. Paul employed the book three times. Habakkuk 1:5 served Paul in Acts 13: 41:

> 'Look, you scoffers, wonder and perish, for I am going to do something in your days that you would never believe, even if someone told you.'

This passage Paul recited to the Jews in Antioch. Habakkuk meant the coming exile, but Paul meant the good news of Jesus conquering death. This was another example of a second meaning being greater than the first meaning for Christians.

A portion of Habakkuk 2:4, 'my righteous one will live by faith', was used by Paul twice—in Romans 1:17 and in Galatians 3:11. It became the rallying cry hundreds of years later for Protestantism. The righteous are justified not by the Law or by their good works, but they are justified by faith. Hebrews 10:37–38 applied Habakkuk 2:4 as well as the preceding verse 3:

> For in just a very little while, "He who is coming will come and will not delay. But my righteous one will live by faith..."

Habakkuk referred to the captives who would be exiled in Babylon. Believers must persevere. The book of Hebrews used it also for perseverance—but for the believers in Christ.

Zechariah prophesied after the exile. His book was a favorite source for Jesus and his followers, being drawn upon four times. Zechariah's Messianic prophesies in chapters 9 through 13 yielded all four quotes. In Mark 14:27 Jesus himself recited Zechariah 13:7 to his disciples on the Mount of Olives:

> "You will all fall away," Jesus told them, "for it is written:
> 'I will strike the shepherd, and the sheep will be scattered.'

Zechariah referred to the Messiah and the restoration of Israel. After the Last Supper Jesus alluded to his crucifixion and the cowardice of his disciples. Peter declared he would die with Christ and the other disciples agreed. But Jesus and prophecy prevailed.

Both John 12:15 and Matthew 21:5 made use of Zechariah 9:9. The most complete quote was in Matthew 21:4–5:

> This took place to fulfill what was spoken through the prophet:
> "Say to the Daughter of Zion, 'See, your king comes to you, gentle and riding on a donkey, on a colt, the foal of a donkey.'"

Again, this was Messianic prophecy by Zechariah, fulfilled—as Matthew noted—by the triumphant entry of Jesus into Jerusalem on a donkey.

John 19:37 applied Zechariah 12:10: "They will look on the one they have pierced." John witnessed the dreadful event during the crucifixion of Jesus that fulfilled this Messianic prophecy of Zechariah. A Roman soldier, making certain Jesus was dead on the cross, thrust a spear into his side.

Matthew 27:9–10 loosely quoted Zechariah 11:12–13:

> Then what was spoken by Jeremiah the prophet was fulfilled: "They took the thirty silver coins, the price set on him by the people of Israel, and they used them to buy the potter's field, as the Lord commanded me."

This was the grim fate of Judas' payment for his betrayal. Judas had already died by his own hand. The Jewish priests used his thirty silver coins to buy a potter's field for burying strangers. Although the narrative of Matthew attributes the quote to Jeremiah it fits more closely the same prophecy in the book of Zechariah.[53] In context, Zechariah used it for the breakdown of the covenant between God and the Jews.

Among the Twelve, the tiny book of Joel contributed two quotes to the New Testament. In Acts 2:17-21 Peter recited God's promise of the Holy Spirit from Joel 2:28-32:

> I will pour out my Spirit on all people.
> Your sons and daughters will prophesy, your young men will see visions, your old men will dream dreams.
> Even on my servants, both men and women, I will pour out my Spirit in those days, and they will prophesy.
> I will show wonders in the heaven above and signs on the earth below, blood and fire and billows of smoke.
> The sun will be turned to darkness and the moon to blood before the coming of the great and glorious day of the Lord.
> And everyone who calls on the name of the Lord will be saved.

Joel prophesied an outpouring of the Holy Spirit in a time of great trouble. Peter used this long quote in his speech at the Temple on the day of Pentecost. The last verse of the quotation Paul also employed, in Romans 10:13: "Everyone who calls on the name of the Lord will be saved."

Twice the followers of Jesus quoted the book of Amos, a forerunner of Isaiah, in the New Testament. Stephen recalled Amos 5:25-27 in Acts 7:42-43:

> This agrees with what is written in the book of the prophets:
> 'Did you bring me sacrifices and offerings forty years in the desert, O house of Israel?
> You have lifted up the shrine of Molech and the star of your god Rephan, the idols you made to worship.
> Therefore I will send you into exile beyond Babylon.

Stephen quoted the passage to the Sanhedrin as part of his proof that Israel always rejected its prophets. Later in his speech (Acts 7:51), he cried, "You always resist the Holy Spirit!" The result was Stephen's execution by stoning.

In Acts 15:16–17 James, the half-brother of Jesus, recited Amos 9:11–12:

> "After this I will return and rebuild David's fallen tent.
> Its ruins I will rebuild, and I will restore it, that the remnant of men may seek the Lord, and all the Gentiles who bear my name, says the Lord, who does these things"

Again, Amos had referred to the Babylonian exile. But James employed Amos to recommend waiving certain Jewish legalisms for the Gentiles. James was in Jerusalem with Peter, Paul, Barnabas and other followers of Jesus debating how they should evangelize the Gentiles.

The New Testament contains two quotations from the book of Micah, a prophet contemporary with Isaiah. Micah 7:6 served Jesus in Matthew 10:35–36:

> For I have come to turn 'a man against his father, a daughter against her mother, a daughter-in-law against her mother-in-law — a man's enemies will be the members of his own household.'

Micah, anticipating the captivity, prophesied great trials ahead for the Jews. Jesus was warning his followers they would experience similar great difficulties, even within their own families.

In Matthew 2:6 the chief priests and teachers of the law used the words of God from Micah 5:2 to answer King Herod's question about where the Messiah was prophesied to be born:

> 'But you, Bethlehem, in the land of Judah, are by no means least among the rulers of Judah; for out of you will come a ruler who will be the shepherd of my people Israel.'

Micah prophesied a ruler who never materialized until the birth of Jesus. It was definitely Messianic because the rest of Micah 5:2 (not quoted in Matthew) read 'whose origins are from of old, from ancient times'.

Malachi also prophesied after the exile. The followers of Jesus made use of the book of Malachi twice. The quote of Malachi 3:1 virtually opened the Gospel of Mark (Mark 1:2):

> It is written in Isaiah the prophet:
> "I will send my messenger ahead of you, who will prepare your way"

In context Malachi may have been referring to himself. But to the followers of Jesus it was prophecy fulfilled by John the Baptist, the messenger for the Messiah. This is also an example of what seems a wrong attribution. But the quote from Malachi is immediately followed by a quote from Isaiah.

Malachi 1:2–3 Paul employed in Romans 9:13: "Just as it is written: 'Jacob I loved, but Esau I hated.'" Here Paul quoted Scriptures to emphasize God was sovereign. Paul went on to ask in the next verse, "What then shall we say? Is God unjust?" He answered himself, "Not at all." It was not for men to judge God's actions. And if God chose to save the Gentiles too, the Jews were not to question it — any more than they could question the selection of Jacob over Esau.

The book of Haggai accounts for one quotation in the New Testament. Hebrews 12:26 recalled Haggai 2:6:

> At that time his voice shook the earth, but now he has promised, "Once more I will shake not only the earth but also the heavens."

Haggai prophesied after the Jews returned to Israel from exile. Some thought the destruction of Jerusalem in 70 AD fulfilled Haggai's prophecy. But the writer of Hebrews reasoned it was an end-times prophecy. In Hebrews 12:28 he urged the faithful to thank God "with reverence and awe", so that they would gain "a kingdom that cannot be shaken".

In summary, the Twelve prophets were very significant to Jesus and his followers, being quoted 25 times — fully 10 percent of the Old Testament quotations in the New Testament!

Now proceed to the remaining writings and prophets…

< 17 >

MORE WRITINGS JESUS AND HIS FOLLOWERS LOVED

The Pentateuch, the book of Psalms, the book of Isaiah and the 'Twelve' account for 225 of the 247 quotations of the Old Testament in the New Testament by Jesus and his followers — a robust 91 percent! But they loved other Jewish Scriptures too. Among the 'Writings' Jesus and his followers overwhelmingly favored the book of Psalms but they also quoted other Writings, 10 times in fact. These other Writings were Job, Daniel and Proverbs. Yes, Daniel. As noted in Chapter 3, although today Daniel is considered one of the 'prophets', the ancient Jews included Daniel in the 'Writings'.

Examine Daniel first. Jesus made use of a phrase from Daniel 9:27 (also 11:31 and 12:11 in Daniel) in Mark 13:14:

> When you see 'the abomination that causes desolation' standing where it does not belong — let the reader understand — then let those who are in Judea flee to the mountains.

This was the response of Jesus to his disciples' question, "what will be the sign of your coming and of the end of the age?" His coming would be preceded by terrible persecution, signaled by an abomination in the holy place. Some have interpreted that event — prophesied by Daniel in about 600 BC — as the Roman destruction of the Temple in 70 AD. But because Jesus seemed to say in Mark that the terrible times are dependent on his 'second coming', many scholars believe the prophecy is yet to be fulfilled.

John cited Daniel 7:13 in his book of Revelations 1:13–14:

> and among the lampstands was someone "like a son of man," dressed in a robe reaching down to his feet and with a golden sash around his chest. His head and hair were white like wool, as white as snow, and his eyes were like blazing fire.

Although the prophet Ezekiel repeatedly used the phrase 'son of man', he applied it to himself. John in his book of Revelations almost certainly alluded to Daniel's use of the term. John's description of the 'son of man' that followed his use of the term matched Daniel's description of God in Daniel 7:9, "the hair of his head was white like wool".

Paul twice drew upon the book of Job, that great story of steadfast faith. Paul used Job 5:13 in 1 Corinthians 3:19:

> For the wisdom of this world is foolishness in God's sight. As it is written: "He catches the wise in their craftiness"...

These were the words of Job's friend Eliphaz, counseling Job during his trials. These words from the book of Job constitute just one quote of several Old Testament quotes in this part of Paul's letter, which emphasized the futility of human wisdom.

In Romans 11:35 Paul employed Job again, this time 41:11: "Who has ever given to God, that God should repay him?" Here Paul was speaking of God's gifts to mankind. What has man done for God to receive these gifts? In Job these words were spoken by God himself.

So Jesus and his followers made use of Daniel and Job four times. But of all the Writings other than the book of Psalms the book most loved by the followers of Jesus was the book of Proverbs. Although Jesus himself did not quote Proverbs, his followers quoted it seven times. The writer of the letter to the Hebrews used it twice.

Hebrews 12:4–6 employed Proverbs 3:11–12 in its last two verses:

> In your struggle against sin, you have not yet resisted to the point of shedding your blood. And you have forgotten that word of encouragement that addresses you as sons:
> "My son, do not make light of the Lord's discipline, and do not lose heart when he rebukes you, because the Lord disciplines those he loves, and he punishes everyone he accepts as a son."

Here the writer reminded the faithful that they had not yet suffered like Jesus, then cited Proverbs to show them that disciplining was an act of love.

Hebrews 12:13 quoted Proverbs 4:26: "Make level paths for your feet." This again referred to discipline, 'walk the straight-and-narrow', so to speak. The writer to the Hebrews quickly added in the next verse, "Make every effort to live in peace with all men and to be holy; without holiness no one will see the Lord."

Both Peter in 1 Peter 5:5 and James, half-brother of Jesus, in James 4:6 used Proverbs 3:34 — in identical words: "God opposes the proud but gives grace to the humble." Again, this was a proverb used for righteousness, as well as good advice for living in peace with others.

Peter also made use of Proverbs 11:31 in 1 Peter 4:18:

> "If it is hard for the righteous to be saved, what will become of the ungodly and the sinner?"

Peter had just made the point that suffering as a Christian was hard but unbelievers and sinners would suffer much more at the judgment.

Peter employed yet another proverb in 2 Peter 2:22: "A dog returns to its vomit." Here Peter applied this powerful metaphor of Proverb 26:11 to backsliding and warned of terrible consequences. He who knew what was right and still returned to sin was more evil in God's eyes than one who was ignorant.

Paul quoted Proverbs 25:21-22 in Romans 12:20:

> On the contrary: 'If your enemy is hungry, feed him; if he is thirsty, give him something to drink.
> In doing this, you will heap burning coals on his head.'

This passage occurred after Paul urged the Christians of Rome not to take revenge. The last sentence in the quotation from Proverbs is often misunderstood. 'Heaping burning coals' did not mean cynical manipulation of an enemy. The context would not allow that. Paul used it in a sense unknown today. Paul's use of the metaphor undoubtedly referred to an ancient Middle East ritual in which one carried a bowl of glowing embers on top of the head to show repentance.[54] Paul actually said then that if you are kind to your enemies, they will repent.

The ancient Jews regarded the book of Proverbs as the tome of rules for getting along with others. It seemed in no way Messianic. So why did the followers of Jesus quote it so often? It is noteworthy that the followers quoted proverbs that develop righteousness for God, concentrated in chapters 2 through 4 and 25 through 29. It is significant that only one time did they draw upon what is called 'The Main Collection of Solomon's Proverbs' (Proverbs 10 through 22:16), a collection aimed at the business of life. Even that one time — quoting Proverbs 11:31 — had to do with righteousness.

Now consider the Writings that Jesus and his followers shunned...

< 18 >

WRITINGS JESUS AND HIS FOLLOWERS SHUNNED

Why did Jesus and his followers completely shun certain 'Writings'? Of the quotes found in the New Testament from the books of the Writings, not one comes from Ruth, Esther, Ecclesiastes, Song of Songs, Lamentations, Ezra, Nehemiah or the Chronicles. Of these books, largest by far is the Chronicles (today divided into two books). Chronicles draws on earlier Jewish Scriptures, with as much as half the material coming from Samuel and Kings. It is reasonable to think these books would not have been favorites for pious Jews to memorize, since they contained so much redundant material.

The other neglected Writings were not large books like the Chronicles, but only Ruth could be considered a tiny book like some of the books of the minor prophets. No, size here seemed not a consideration. What is the common thread? Could style be a factor even though many scholars have always considered Song of Songs superior poetry? Could wisdom be a factor even though Ecclesiastes has been the favorite of weary cynics for ages? No, lack of style and wisdom are not credible reasons.

Consider the shunned Writings one by one.

Ruth is more than a skilful short story of redemption. It was a book of importance. After all, Ruth was a Moabite—a Gentile—who through patience and devotion to her Jewish mother-in-law Naomi met her future husband Boaz. Sturdy, decent Ruth became the great grandmother of David. So Jews revered her name. In fact her name is listed in the lineage of Jesus in Matthew 1:5. The book of Ruth however contains not one prophecy, let alone a prophecy of the Messiah.

Esther also tells an inspiring story. Esther was the reverse of Ruth, being a Jew among Gentiles (in her case, Persians). The book of Esther has been challenged as to its validity as Holy Scripture (often called 'canonicity'). Esther like Ruth however has much merit, both as inspiration and as skilled literature. But Esther is truly unique, according to

John Walvoord, in that it does not directly refer to God, worship, prayer, sacrifice or prophecy.[55] Naturally there is no Messianic tone to the book at all. The name Esther occurs nowhere in the New Testament. In fact, outside the book of Esther the name Esther occurs nowhere in the Old Testament.

Ecclesiastes — traditionally a product of Solomon's hand — has been favored by sophisticates like Ernest Hemingway because of its weary cynicism. A reader can almost hear the author sigh from 3000 years ago, "Life has no meaning." Most scholars agree the consistent message of Ecclesiastes is that life has no ultimate value.[56] No matter what a person accomplishes or does not accomplish that person is going to die anyway. That person is going to be forgotten like all the others before. Nor does it matter if a person is righteous or sinful. No one is rewarded or punished in this life. Or afterward. The dismal teaching of Ecclesiastes is much like the beliefs of existentialists of today.

Only the last few verses of Ecclesiastes offer any hope that God would judge the deeds of mankind. But the verses seemed 'tacked on'. C. S. Lewis tried to cope with the gloomy message of Ecclesiastes and understand why it was considered sacred.[57] Not willing to give up on it, he concluded that it is a masterpiece depicting the futility of a man's life separated from God. If nothing else it represents some kind of sophisticated paganism in that it does advance certain truths. But this generous justification by Lewis for including Ecclesiastes in the Bible scarcely applied to the spiritual world of Jesus and his followers. They totally ignored the book.

Song of Songs — suspected also of being written by Solomon — has also been a favorite of sophisticates for its sensuality. It is a 'love poem' about a man and a woman. In its spiritual defense one can value its emphasis on fidelity and its depiction of the profound depth of romantic love. Some however delve into its more sensuous passages, anxious to explain what physical activity or body part lies behind each metaphor. They are much like chemists analyzing pigments used by Rembrandt, as if that will explain his great art. Still, whatever analyses scholars of today make they do not change the fact that Song of Songs contains no prophecy of any kind. Jesus and his followers did not quote or allude to the Song of Songs at all in the New Testament.

Lamentations was a short book bemoaning the fall of Jerusalem to the invading Babylonians and the subsequent destruction of the Temple. The book is cleverly constructed acrostic poetry. In acrostic poetry each successive line begins with the next letter of the Hebrew alphabet. Scholars have always suspected Jeremiah wrote Lamentations. But that great prophet did not invest Lamentations with his prophecy. The book is an outpouring of grief, a lament. Jesus and his followers ignored the book completely.

Ezra is a book about resettling Israel after the exile in Babylon. Nehemiah is a book about rebuilding city walls around Jerusalem. The events in the books were virtually contemporaneous. Both are fine stories and historically important. But they do not brim with the kind of inspiration Jesus and his followers sought. Ezra and Nehemiah differ from Ruth and Esther however in that they at least each have one prophecy about God's eternal love for Israel. Still, Jesus and followers shunned Ezra and Nehemiah. Neither occurs in the New Testament.

Yet another possibility remains for why these particular Writings were shunned. Modern scholars might never have suspected this possibility had the Jamnia synod not been held a few years after the Romans destroyed Jerusalem in 70 AD. At Jamnia (about 30 miles west of Jerusalem) Johanan ben Zakkai led other Jewish scholars in a discussion of the canonicity of Jewish Scriptures. In other words, which books were truly inspired by God? The scholars questioned four books in particular. Three of them were from the Writings: Esther, Ecclesiastes and Song of Songs.

Although the synod did not ultimately exclude the three from Jewish Scriptures it seems plausible that pious Jews of the time of Jesus only reluctantly accepted Esther, Ecclesiastes and Song of Songs. Also at that time Jews probably had little interest in the redundancies of Chronicles. So likewise, Christians budding from Jewish roots had little interest in those four books, nor in Ruth, Lamentations, Ezra or Nehemiah. These latter four books offered scarcely any prophecy and certainly no Messianic prophecy.

Ironically, five of these books became the 'five festal scrolls or the 'Megilloth' used in Jewish festivals: Song of Songs, recited at Passover; Ruth, used in the Festival of Weeks; Lamentations, commemorating the fall of Jerusalem; Ecclesiastes, associated with the feast of Tabernacles; and Esther, read at Purim. This festival usage virtually guaranteed their permanent canonicity.

Next, consider the prophets other than Isaiah that Jesus and his followers loved…

< 19 >

OTHER PROPHETS JESUS AND HIS FOLLOWERS LOVED

This chapter discusses more prophets (other than Isaiah and 'the Twelve') loved by Jesus and his followers. Of these, Jeremiah, one of the 'latter prophets' (which also includes Isaiah) is very significant. Jesus and his followers quoted Jeremiah six times in the New Testament. Jeremiah was born several decades after the death of Isaiah. The Assyrians were no longer a threat to Israel. But Israel's conquest by Babylon was imminent. Jeremiah escaped exile in Babylon but he had to flee eventually to Egypt (where he subsequently died). The book attributed to Jeremiah is one of the most voluminous of the Bible. It carries much Messianic significance.

To a crowd at the Temple in Jerusalem Jesus made use of Jeremiah 7:11 (preceded by a quote of Isaiah 56:7) to explain why he drove out the merchants. Mark 11:17 recorded:

> And as he taught them, he said, "Is it not written:
> 'My house will be called a house of prayer for all nations'?
> But you have made it 'a den of robbers'."

Jeremiah had condemned the sinful Jews of his time, who were virtually hiding in the Temple as if it gave them protection. On the other hand Jesus condemned the crass commercialism in the Temple. The money changers and those selling animals for sacrifice had made his 'Father's House of Prayer' into 'a den of robbers'.

Paul employed Jeremiah 9:24 twice, in 1 Corinthians 1:31 and 2 Corinthians 10:17: "Let him who boasts boast in the Lord." Jeremiah was lamenting the ingratitude of the Jews. At times, beleaguered Paul had to defend his ministry, even boast of his accomplishments, but boasting grated against his belief. For Paul knew all the things happening to him and the other followers of Jesus were though God's grace.

Matthew 2:17–19 drew upon Jeremiah 31:15:

> Then what was said through the prophet Jeremiah was fulfilled:
> "A voice is heard in Ramah, weeping and great mourning,
>   Rachel weeping for her children and refusing to be com-
>   forted, because they are no more."

Ramah, just north of Jerusalem, was a village through which the Jews of Jerusalem passed on their way to exile in Babylon. Matthew saw a second meaning, a terrible prophecy fulfilled by King Herod's murderous purge of all boys two years old and younger. Joseph and Mary of course had already fled to Egypt with the object of Herod's search — the infant Jesus.

Hebrews 8:8–12 used Jeremiah 31:31–34 for yet another Messianic prophecy:

> "The time is coming, declares the Lord, when I will make a new covenant with the house of Israel and with the house of Judah.
> It will not be like the covenant I made with their forefathers when I took them by the hand to lead them out of Egypt, because they did not remain faithful to my covenant, and I turned away from them, declares the Lord.
> This is the covenant I will make with the house of Israel after that time, declares the Lord.
> I will put my laws in their minds and write them on their hearts.
> I will be their God, and they will be my people.
> No longer will a man teach his neighbor, or a man his brother, saying, 'Know the Lord,' because they will all know me, from the least of them to the greatest.
> For I will forgive their wickedness and will remember their sins no more."

The writer of the book of Hebrews was citing nothing less than Jeremiah's prophecy for a new covenant with the Messiah. Paul also quoted Jeremiah 31:33–34 in a shortened form in Romans 11:27. Paul meant that the Jews of the old covenant were not lost — if they received the new covenant.

Five quotes found in the New Testament were from the books of the ' former prophets', the group that included Joshua, Judges, Samuel and Kings. Jesus certainly alluded to David and other heroic figures in the books of Samuel and Kings. However Jesus never quoted the former prophets. Paul accounts for four of the five quotes of the former prophets by the followers of Jesus.

Paul used 2 Samuel 7:14 in 2 Corinthians 6:18:

> "I will be a Father to you, and you will be my sons and daughters, says the Lord Almighty."

God spoke these words in 2 Samuel to Nathan, who relayed them to David. Paul applied the quote to fledgling Christians, who were to be the children of God. Hebrews 1:5 also used 2 Samuel 7:14, in that case to prove God condoned the supremacy of the Messiah Jesus — the offspring of David — over all. Part of the verse preceding 2 Samuel 7:14 read: 'I will establish the throne of his kingdom forever'. It is clear the followers of Jesus considered these verses Messianic prophecy.

2 Samuel 22:50 served Paul in Romans 15:9:

> "Therefore I will praise you among the Gentiles; I will sing hymns to your name."

Does this passage in 2 Samuel sound familiar? It has been mentioned before. Perhaps written by David, it is also Psalm 18.[58] 'Praise among the Gentiles' was of course a familiar refrain for Paul. He was always assuring Gentiles that the good news of the Jewish Messiah rising from the dead was relevant to them.

Paul applied 1 Kings 19:10 and 1 Kings 19:18 in succession in these passages from Romans 11:2–4:

> God did not reject his people, whom he foreknew. Don' t you know what the Scripture says in the passage about Elijah — how he appealed to God against Israel: "Lord, they have killed your prophets and torn down your altars; I am the only one left, and they are trying to kill me"? And what was God's answer to him? "I have reserved for myself seven thousand who have not bowed the knee to Baal."

Here Paul quoted passages of 1 Kings to answer the question of whether or not God had rejected the Israelites. No, by God's grace a remnant of the chosen still remained.

Jesus and his followers loved the preceding prophets. But what of the prophets that Jesus and his followers shunned?

Consider the shunned prophets next…

< 20 >

PROPHETS JESUS AND HIS FOLLOWERS SHUNNED

Why did Jesus and his followers seem to completely shun certain prophets?

This consideration is almost as illuminating for a Christian as considering the prophets Jesus and his followers did love. Of the five quotes found in the New Testament from the books of the 'former prophets', none was from Joshua and Judges. Is there a good reason for this? Consider the nature of Joshua and Judges. From the end of the Pentateuch they recorded continuous history of the Jews from Joshua's conquest of the 'promised land' Canaan to Samuel's birth just before the advent of Israeli kings. This 300 years contained heroic stories: Joshua, Gideon, Deborah, Samson and others. But Jesus never even mentioned the name of Joshua, Gideon, Deborah, Samson or anyone else in the books of Joshua and Judges. However, the mention of these heroes in Hebrews 11:32 is enlightening:

> And what more shall I say? I do not have time to tell about Gideon, Barak, Samson, Jephthah, David, Samuel and the prophets…

Jesus and his followers had good news — the Gospel — to spread far and wide. And not much time. The good news was the Messiah and salvation. Nothing in Joshua and Judges was considered Messianic.

Among the Twelve (today's 'minor prophets'), Obadiah, Jonah, Nahum and Zephaniah contributed no quotes. These were tiny books. Obadiah, a mere 600 or so words, is a diatribe against Edom. The earlier chapter in this book on the Psalms discussed the extreme anger of Jews toward Edom. Edomites were descendants of Esau who lived in the mountains to the southeast. They rankled the Jews as no other neighbors did. Perhaps it was their smugness in believing they were invulnerable in their mountain stronghold. But more likely it was their gloating over Israel's troubles. During the Babylonian captivity they even took some Israeli land. Regardless of cause, Obadiah's rage against Edom was probably of scant interest to Jesus and his followers.

In a similar vein Nahum in 1100 angry words condemned the Assyrian city of Nineveh. Nahum called for its destruction. No doubt in the eyes of the Jews this capital of the Assyrian oppressors deserved condemnation and destruction. But nothing in the book was Messianic. This rage from an ancient time against an empire that had subsequently collapsed was probably a subject of little interest to Jesus and his followers.

Zephaniah contains about 1500 words. The prophet was a contemporary of Nahum. He was privileged, being a descendant of King Hezekiah. It is significant that Zephaniah prophesied the coming judgment against Israel as well as the hope for a remnant. In many ways Zephaniah's book of prophecy was similar to the great prophetic books of Jeremiah and Isaiah. Why did Zephaniah not appeal to Jesus and his followers? It can only be speculated that the other prophets said it better, for 'remnant' was a common theme. Also, Zephaniah had not one prophecy considered Messianic.

The book of Jonah is tiny too, about 1200 words. Jonah was probably a contemporary of Hosea, Joel, Amos, Obadiah and Micah. As a Messianic prophet he paled beside Hosea and Micah. Even so, the absence of quotes from the prophet is puzzling. His experience inside the great fish for three days foreshadowed Christ's entombment and resurrection. Nevertheless, for that very reason Jesus did allude to (but not quote) Jonah in Matthew 12:39-41.

Now consider the most puzzling exclusion of all: why did Jesus and his followers completely neglect the prophet Ezekiel? Ezekiel is a major book in the Old Testament. It contains nearly 40,000 words. In pure volume it exceeds Genesis or Isaiah. In pure volume it exceeds the entire collection of the Twelve (today's 'minor prophets'). In fact the book of Ezekiel is exceeded in size only by the Psalms and Jeremiah. Ezekiel had astonishing visions. He made end-time prophecies embraced by many later scholars. His message of God's sovereignty is noble. Ezekiel even has one long passage — chapter 34 — considered Messianic. Yet Ezekiel was shunned by Jesus and his followers. Why?

Comparison of Ezekiel to the prophets Isaiah and Jeremiah yields a number of possible reasons. Stylistically Ezekiel is unpleasing compared to the other two. Isaiah and Jeremiah wrote largely in poetry, rich in images. Ezekiel wrote prose, hammering and legalistic. Poetry is much easier to memorize than prose. Perhaps most important though was the fact that Ezekiel was much less Messianic than the other two. John Walvoord attributes one Messianic prophecy to Ezekiel whereas Jeremiah had five and Isaiah had 31.[59]

But what of the one undeniable Messianic prophesy in Ezekiel's chapter 34? The long passage develops a shepherd metaphor. The trusting flock of Israel had been betrayed by bad shepherds. God declared he would shepherd the people of Israel. In Ezekiel 34:23 God goes on to say, "I will place over them one shepherd, my servant David, and he will tend them..." Why didn't Jesus and his followers seize on this wonderful prophecy? The answer is not obvious in the context of Ezekiel. But it is obvious when compared to Jeremiah. For Jeremiah 23 made the same prophecy. Israel had been betrayed by bad shepherds. God declared he would shepherd the people of Israel. In Jeremiah 23:5 God says, "I will raise up to David a righteous Branch, a King who will reign wisely and do what is just and right in the land." Ezekiel then is another example of a prophet neglected because someone else — in his case, Jeremiah — said the same thing but said it better.

Yet another possibility remains for the exclusion of Ezekiel. At the Jamnia synod in 70 AD the Jewish scholars challenged four books in particular as being uninspired Jewish Scriptures. Three were Esther, Ecclesiastes and Song of Songs. But perhaps the greatest controversy was over Ezekiel. The prophet not only had prophesied things which seemed historically untrue but on some issues he disagreed with the Pentateuch — the 'Law'. The synod did not conclude Ezekiel was not God's revelation. But the fact that they debated Ezekiel suggests many Jews in the time of Jesus harbored doubts about the book. Under the circumstances, would Ezekiel have been a good source to quote for evangelizing? The answer seems obvious. Besides, Jeremiah had delivered the same Messianic message but had done it so much better.

In summary, mainly because of no Messianic messages Jesus and his followers shunned Ezekiel, Obadiah, Jonah, Nahum and Zephaniah. But a contributing factor may also have been that another prophet said the same thing but said it much better.

Now at last, consider how a Christian of today can use all the observations in the preceding chapters to study the Bible...

< 21 >

A BOLD PLAN TO LOVE THE BIBLE JESUS LOVED

The study of the Old Testament is daunting, so daunting it just doesn't get done very often. Sandra Richter expounds on this study as the 'dysfunctional closet'.[60] The Old Testament is the cluttered closet no one has time to put in order. The Old Testament is three times longer than the New Testament. Who has time for such a task? It is hard enough to find time to study the New Testament. Still, the spirits of the Christian saints nag us to try.

Here is a plan.

Is it rational for the Christian to spend twice as much time studying 1 and 2 Kings in the Old Testament as studying Matthew in the New Testament? Of course not. That is obvious to a Christian. It is less obvious but still irrational for a Christian studying the Old Testament to spend as much time studying Ezekiel as studying Isaiah. In view of what we have learned in the preceding chapters there is a logical and defensible way to study the Old Testament.

THE LOGIC

The way through the Old Testament is illuminated by Jesus and his followers. Preferences of Jesus and his followers for specific books of the Old Testament light the path for Christians making their way through the Old Testament. Yes, the preceding chapters reveal which books the Old Testament Jesus and his followers loved. So the Christian reader may allocate study time according to how well Jesus and his followers loved certain books of the Old Testament.

It is completely logical and defensible for the Christian reader to allocate time to the three Old Testament divisions as follows: 33 percent to the Law, 38 percent to the Prophets and 29 percent to the Writings. And within those three divisions the Christian reader may also allocate time based on how well Jesus and his followers loved specific books. Of course the allocation must not be applied slavishly with

mathematical exactitude. That approach would result in complete neglect of numerous books 'shunned' by Jesus and his followers. These
books need attention—however brief—for a real survey of the Old
Testament by the Christian of today.

Consider this allocation within the Law's 33 percent: Genesis 50
percent, Exodus-Deuteronomy 40 percent, Leviticus 7 percent and
Numbers 3 percent. It is hard to overemphasize Genesis or Exodus-
Deuteronomy. Genesis laid the foundation for creation, the nature of
God, the nature of mankind, salvation and covenants. In short, Genesis
introduces virtually every major Old Testament theme, even hinting at
the Messiah in several passages.[61] Exodus, Deuteronomy and Leviticus
are important in that they were the heart of the Jewish law. On the
other hand, study Numbers much the same way as other books of Jewish history (like 1 and 2 Samuel), respectfully but not expecting profound developments of Old Testament themes.

Now consider this allocation within the Prophets' 38 percent. The
former prophets Joshua, Judges, Samuel and Kings (six Old Testament
books) receive about 10 percent, primarily to examine the life of David.
The other 90 percent is allotted to the latter prophets Isaiah, Jeremiah,
Ezekiel and the 'Twelve' (Hosea, Joel, Amos, Obadiah, Jonah, Micah,
Nahum, Habakkuk, Zephaniah, Haggai, Zechariah and Malachi). But
half of the 90 percent goes to Isaiah alone! A thorough study of Isaiah
is a must for understanding what this prophet offered Jesus and his
followers. Next in import are Jeremiah, Hosea, Zechariah and Habakkuk with 5 percent each. Joel, Amos, Micah, Haggai and Malachi share
15 percent. The five prophets Jesus and his followers shunned—
Ezekiel, Obadiah, Jonah, Nahum and Zephaniah—receive the remaining 5 percent.

Lastly, allocate the 29 percent for the Writings. Psalms over-
whelms the other writings. Allot two-thirds of the 29 percent for
Psalms, about 10 percent for Proverbs and 5.5 percent each for Daniel
and Job. The remaining 10 or so percent is sprinkled among Ruth,
Esther, Lamentations, Ecclesiastes, Song of Songs, Ezra, Nehemiah and
Chronicles. This latter allocation may seem very meager but in reality
it gives these Scriptures more emphasis than Jesus and his followers
apparently gave them.

THE DETAIL

Next apply these percentages to an ambitious but realistic one-year study of the Old Testament. Assume five hours of study per week for 50 weeks, or 250 hours for the year. *This approach primarily allocates study time.* For study purposes, scant consideration is given below to what can be attained for a particular book in that amount of time. Various depths of study are noted. Consult Appendix B for a review of the fundamentals of Bible study. Is time sufficient to perform both 'exegesis' (digesting the book's message to its contemporaries) and 'hermeneutics' (used here to mean deciphering the book's message to readers of today)? Is time sufficient to cogitate on the book's message to Jesus and his followers? Or is there only time to read the book briskly and to grasp its overall message? Beware: in some cases even a brisk reading is not possible in the time allowed!

Remember: the following is primarily a guide to *allotting time*, not a plan on how to study each book.

THE LAW   (83 HOURS):

Genesis   (43 hours)
The time seems generous but the reader will need every minute to digest the book's message to the Jews who lived it, to the Jews in the time of Jesus and to the reader of today. Study Creation though the Patriarchs, and the birth of the twelve tribes of Israel.

Exodus   (17 hours)
Enjoy and reflect on the story of Moses. Rigorous study is required too, for the story introduces the basis of morality, the Ten Commandments.

Leviticus   (5 hours)
Study how the Jews established their priestly ways.

Numbers   (3 hours)
Read an overview of this large book with over 30,000 words, study the structure of the book and sample some passages. Get the sense of history of Moses in the desert.

Deuteronomy   (15 hours)

Ample time is given to ruminate on the commandments and God's judgment on all the original refugees from Egypt. Enjoy and reflect on the various laws and covenants. This book concludes the foundation of the Jewish nation.

THE PROPHETS   (95 HOURS):

Joshua	(1.0 hours)
Judges	(1.0 hours)
1 Samuel	(2.5 hours)
2 Samuel	(3.5 hours)
1 Kings	(2.0 hours)
2 Kings	(1.0 hours)

From Joshua through 2 Kings the reader has only 11 hours to read 135,000 words. Not only must the reader cope with that volume but also digest 800 years of history (from the death of Moses to the time of captivity in Babylon). Read an overview of these books. Sample some passages. Focus on David. This effort is skimpy, and the reader will encounter these events again and again in the other prophets.

Isaiah   (43 hours)

The time is not excessive. The reader will need every minute to digest and analyze the book's message to the Jews who lived it, to the Jews in the time of Jesus and to the reader of today. Breeze though chapters 30 through 39 but the rest of Isaiah should be studied rigorously. Marvel at the accuracy of the prophecy. Reflect that 700 years would pass before the ministry of the Messiah began. What prophecies in Isaiah are yet unfulfilled?

Jeremiah   (5.5 hours)

Read briskly and selectively this large book with over 40,000 words. Study passages Jesus and his followers quoted.

Ezekiel   (2 hours)

Such a large book can not be read in two hours. Read and reflect on the overview, then read Ezekiel 34:11–31. Why did Jesus and his followers not quote this passage?

Hosea   (5.5 hours)

This book is short yet full of significance for Jesus and his follow-ers. This book deserves the full treatment: digest the book's message to the Jews who lived it, to the Jews in the time of Jesus and to the reader of today.

Joel   (3 hours)

Study this very short book and reflect on its meaning for Jesus and his followers. What meaning does it have for Christians of today?

Amos   (3 hours)

Read this book of 4000 words. Ponder its meaning for Jesus and his followers. What meaning does it have for Christians of today?

Obadiah   (1 hour)

This is the shortest book of the Old Testament. What meaning did it have for Jesus and his followers? What meaning does it have for Christians of today?

Jonah   (2 hour)

Read and digest this well-known story of 1300 words. It seems so Messianic, yet it was never quoted.

Micah   (3 hours)

It is short yet it was full of significance for Jesus and his followers. This book deserves the full treatment: digest the book's message to the Jews who lived it, to the Jews in the time of Jesus and to the reader of today.

Nahum   (1 hour)

Read this short book and reflect on its meaning.

Habakkuk   (4.5 hours)

This book is very short yet it was full of significance for Jesus and his followers. This book deserves the full treatment: digest the book's message to the Jews who lived it, to the Jews in the time of Jesus and to the reader of today.

Zephaniah   (1 hour)

Read and reflect on the meaning of this very short poetic book.

Haggai   (3 hours)

Read this very short book and reflect on its meaning for Jesus and his followers. What meaning does it have for Christians of today?

Zechariah   (4.5 hours)
This book is short yet it was full of significance for Jesus and his followers. This book deserves full treatment: digest the book's message to the Jews who lived it, to the Jews in the time of Jesus and to the reader of today.

Malachi   (3 hours)
Read this very short book and reflect on its meaning for Jesus and his followers. What meaning does it have for Christians of today?

THE WRITINGS   (72 HOURS):

Ruth   (1 hour)
1 Chronicles   (1 hour)
2 Chronicles   (1 hour)
Ezra   (1 hour)
Nehemiah   (1 hour)
Esther   (1 hour)

Except for Ruth these books can not be read in one hour. Read a few passages of each one and reflect on the overview.

Job   (4 hours)
Read this well-liked book of 10,000 words and reflect on its meaning for Jesus and his followers. What does it mean for Christians of today?

Psalms   (48 hours)
The time is not excessive. The reader will need every minute to digest and analyze the collection of psalms. Read all the psalms. Read carefully the 39 psalms quoted by Jesus and his followers. Study most thoroughly the 10 psalms that were quoted by Jesus plus psalms 34 and 69.

Proverbs   (7 hours)
Read this book of many proverbs and concentrate on chapters 2 through 4 and 25 through 29. Reflect on their meanings for Jesus and his followers. How are they helpful to today's Christian?

Ecclesiastes	(1 hour)
Song of Songs	(1 hour)
Lamentations	(1 hour)

Read and reflect on their overviews. These books must be read selectively. Read the conclusion in Ecclesiastes 12:13–14. Reflect on the poetry of Song of Songs.

Daniel	(4 hours)

Read this book of 11,000 words diligently and reflect on its meaning for Jesus and his followers. What does it mean for today's Christian?

Choosing to neglect certain books is no more apparent than in the Writings. Can a reader devote a mere hour to Ecclesiastes, a book so loved by modern cynics? Yes, the bold thesis of this study plan is that a Christian is significantly better off studying a few key psalms than the entire book of Ecclesiastes.

THE SUMMARY   (250 HOURS):

In summary, 174 hours of 250 hours are allocated to study the Pentateuch, Isaiah and the Psalms. This is less than the 80 percent of the time that could be reasoned from the proportion of quotes in the New Testament by Jesus and his followers. A small number of hours must be devoted to brief excursions into books that were not quoted at all by Jesus and his followers. Nevertheless this reasoned and weighted method will definitely increase understanding of the Old Testament, Jesus and his followers. Proceed and feel confident that this approach will focus on the important parts of the Old Testament for a Christian. All the great themes of the Old Testament will come forth: God's sovereignty, salvation, flawed mankind, covenants with God, love and the Messiah. And all themes rush on inevitably to fulfillment in one figure. As the disciple Philip cried out joyously in John 1:45:

> We have found the one Moses wrote about in the Law, and about whom the prophets also wrote—Jesus of Nazareth...

APPENDIX A:

QUOTATIONS OF THE OLD TESTAMENT
IN THE NEW TESTAMENT

Quotations gleaned from three compilations:
1. International Bible Society, *The Holy Bible, New International Version* (North American Edition). (Grand Rapids, Michigan: Zondervan, 1984).
2. Nave, Orville J., *Nave's Topical Bible* (Peabody, Massachusetts: Hendrickson Publishers, 1997).
3. Bratcher, Robert G., editor, *Old Testament Quotations in the New Testament*, 3rd ed. (New York: United Bible Societies, 1987).

OLD TESTAMENT	NEW TESTAMENT
Genesis 1:3	2 Corinthians 4:6
Genesis 1:27	Mark 10:6
Genesis 2:2	Hebrews 4:4
Genesis 2:7	1 Corinthians 15:45
Genesis 2:24	Mark 10:7–8
Genesis 2:24	1 Corinthians 6:16
Genesis 2:24	Ephesians 5:31
Genesis 12:1	Acts 7:3
Genesis 12:3	Galatians 3:8
Genesis 12:7	Galatians 3:16
Genesis 15:5	Romans 4:18
Genesis 15:6	Romans 4:3
Genesis 15:6	Galatians 3:6
Genesis 15:6	James 2:23
Genesis 15:13–14	Acts 7:6–7
Genesis 17:5	Romans 4:17
Genesis 18:14	Romans 9:9
Genesis 21:10	Galatians 4:30
Genesis 21:12	Romans 9:7
Genesis 21:12	Hebrews 11:18
Genesis 22:17	Hebrews 6:14
Genesis 22:18	Acts 3:25
Genesis 25:23	Romans 9:12

Genesis 47:31	Hebrews 11:21
Exodus 1:8	Acts 7:18
Exodus 2:13–14	Acts 7:26–28
Exodus 3:5,7,8,10	Acts 7:33–34
Exodus 3:6	Mark 12:26
Exodus 3:6	Acts 7:32
Exodus 9:16	Romans 9:17
Exodus 13:2,13:12	Luke 2:23
Exodus 16:18	2 Corinthians 8:15
Exodus 19:6	1 Peter 2:9
Exodus 20:11	Acts 14:15
Exodus 20:12	Mark 7:10a
Exodus 20:12	Ephesians 6:2–3
Exodus 20:12–16	Mark 10:19
Exodus 20:13	Matthew 5:21
Exodus 20:13–14	James 2:11
Exodus 20:13–17	Romans 13:9
Exodus 20:14	Matthew 5:27
Exodus 20:17	Romans 7:7
Exodus 21:17	Mark 7:10b
Exodus 21:24	Matthew 5:38
Exodus 22:28	Acts 23:5
Exodus 24:8	Hebrews 9:20
Exodus 25:40	Hebrews 8:5
Exodus 32:1	Acts 7:40
Exodus 32:6	1 Corinthians 10:7
Exodus 33:19	Romans 9:15
Exodus 34:33	2 Corinthians 3:13
Leviticus 11:44	1 Peter 1:16
Leviticus 12:8	Luke 2:24
Leviticus 18:5	Romans 10:5
Leviticus 18:5	Galatians 3:12
Leviticus 19:12	Matthew 5:33
Leviticus 19:18	Mark 12:31
Leviticus 19:18	Romans 13:9b
Leviticus 19:18	Galatians 5:14
Leviticus 19:18	James 2:8
Leviticus 26:11–12	2 Corinthians 6:16

Numbers 16:5	2 Timothy 2:19
Deuteronomy 4:24	Hebrews 12:29
Deuteronomy 6:4–5	Mark 12:29–30
Deuteronomy 6:13	Luke 4:8
Deuteronomy 6:16	Luke 4:12
Deuteronomy 8:3	Luke 4:4
Deuteronomy 17:7	1 Corinthians 5:13
Deuteronomy 18:15–19	Acts 3:22–23
Deuteronomy 19:15	Matthew 18:16
Deuteronomy 19:15	2 Corinthians 13:1
Deuteronomy 21:23	Galatians 3:13
Deuteronomy 24:1	Matthew 5:31
Deuteronomy 25:4	1 Corinthians 9:9
Deuteronomy 25:4	1 Timothy 5:18a
Deuteronomy 27:26	Galatians 3:10
Deuteronomy 30:12–14	Romans 10:6–8
Deuteronomy 31:6	Hebrews 13:5
Deuteronomy 32:21	Romans 10:19
Deuteronomy 32:35	Romans 12:19
Deuteronomy 32:35	Hebrews 10:30a
Deuteronomy 32:36	Hebrews 10:30b
Deuteronomy 32:43	Romans 15:10
Deuteronomy 32:43	Hebrews 1:6
2 Samuel 7:14	2 Corinthians 6:18
2 Samuel 7:14	Hebrews 1:5b
2 Samuel 22:50	Romans 15:9
1 Kings 19:10	Romans 11:3
1 Kings 19:18	Romans 11:4
Job 5:13	1 Corinthians 3:19
Job 41:11	Romans 11:35
Psalm 2:1–2	Acts 4:25–26
Psalm 2:7	Acts 13:33
Psalm 2:7	Hebrews 1:5a
Psalm 2:9	Revelations 2:27
Psalm 2:9	Revelations 19:15
Psalm 4:4	Ephesians 4:26
Psalm 5:9	Romans 3:13a

Psalm 6:8	Matthew 7:23
Psalm 8:2	Matthew 21:16
Psalm 8:4–6	Hebrews 2:6–8
Psalm 8:6	1 Corinthians 15:27
Psalm 10:7	Romans 3:14
Psalm 14:3	Romans 3:10–12
Psalm 16:8–11	Acts 2:25–28
Psalm 16:10	Acts 13:35
Psalm 19:4	Romans 10:18
Psalm 22:1	Mark 15:34
Psalm 22:18	Matthew 27:35
Psalm 22:18	John 19:24
Psalm 22:22	Hebrews 2:12
Psalm 24:1	1 Corinthians 10:26
Psalm 31:5	Luke 23:46
Psalm 32:1–2	Romans 4:7–8
Psalm 34:12–16	1 Peter 3:10–12
Psalm 34:20	John 19:36
Psalm 35:19	John 15:25
Psalm 36:1	Romans 3:18
Psalm 40:6–8	Hebrews 10:5–7
Psalm 41:9	John 13:18
Psalm 44:22	Romans 8:36
Psalm 45:6–7	Hebrews 1:8–9
Psalm 51:4	Romans 3:4
Psalm 55:22	1 Peter 5:7
Psalm 62:12	Romans 2:6
Psalm 68:18	Ephesians 4:8
Psalm 69:9	John 2:17
Psalm 69:9	Romans 15:3
Psalm 69:22–23	Romans 11:9–10
Psalm 69:25	Acts 1:20a
Psalm 78:2	Matthew 13:35
Psalm 82:6	John 10:34
Psalm 91:11–12	Luke 4:10–11
Psalm 94:11	1 Corinthians 3:20
Psalm 95:7–11	Hebrews 3:7–11
Psalm 102:25–27	Hebrews 1:10–12
Psalm 104:4	Hebrews 1:7

Psalm 109:8	Acts 1:20b
Psalm 110:1	Mark 12:36
Psalm 110:1	Acts 2:34–35
Psalm 110:1	Hebrews 1:13
Psalm 110:4	Hebrews 5:6
Psalm 112:9	2 Corinthians 9:9
Psalm 116:10	2 Corinthians 4:13
Psalm 117:1	Romans 15:11
Psalm 118:6–7	Hebrews 13:6
Psalm 118:22	1 Peter 2:7
Psalm 118:22–23	Mark 12:10–11
Psalm 118:22–23	Acts 4:11
Psalm 118:26	Mark 11:9
Psalm 140:3	Romans 3:13b
Proverb 3:11–12	Hebrews 12:5–6
Proverb 3:34	James 4:6
Proverb 3:34	1 Peter 5:5
Proverb 4:26	Hebrews 12:13
Proverb 11:31	1 Peter 4:18
Proverb 25:21–22	Romans 12:20
Proverb 26:11	2 Peter 2:22
Isaiah 1:9	Romans 9:29
Isaiah 6:9–10	Mark 4:12
Isaiah 6:9–10	John 12:40–41
Isaiah 6:9–10	Acts 28:25–27
Isaiah 7:14	Matthew 1:23
Isaiah 8:12	1 Peter 3:14
Isaiah 8:14	Romans 9:33a
Isaiah 8:14	1 Peter 2:8
Isaiah 8:17–18	Hebrews 2:13
Isaiah 9:1–2	Matthew 4:15–16
Isaiah 10:22–23	Romans 9:27–28
Isaiah 11:10	Romans 15:12
Isaiah 13:10	Mark 13:24
Isaiah 22:13	1 Corinthians 15:32
Isaiah 25:8	1 Corinthians 15:54
Isaiah 28:11–12	1 Corinthians 14:21
Isaiah 28:16	Romans 9:33b

Isaiah 28:16	1Peter 2:6
Isaiah 29:10	Romans 11:8
Isaiah 29:13	Mark 7:6–7
Isaiah 29:14	1 Corinthians 1:19
Isaiah 29:16	Romans 9:20
Isaiah 34:4	Mark 13:25
Isaiah 40:3	Mark 1:3
Isaiah 40:3	John 1:23
Isaiah 40:3–5	Luke 3:4–6
Isaiah 40:6–8	1 Peter 1:24–25
Isaiah 40:13	Romans 11:34
Isaiah 40:13	1 Corinthians 2:16
Isaiah 42:1–4	Matthew 12:17–21
Isaiah 42:7	Luke 2:32
Isaiah 45:23	Romans 14:11
Isaiah 49:6	Acts 13:47
Isaiah 49:8	2 Corinthians 6:2
Isaiah 52:5	Romans 2:24
Isaiah 52:7	Romans 10:15
Isaiah 52:11	2 Corinthians 6:17
Isaiah 52:15	Romans 15:21
Isaiah 53:1	John 12:38
Isaiah 53:1	Romans 10:16
Isaiah 53:4	Matthew 8:17
Isaiah 53:5–6	1 Peter 2:24–25
Isaiah 53:7–8	Acts 8:32–33
Isaiah 53:9	1 Peter 2:22
Isaiah 53:12	Mark 15:28
Isaiah 54:1	Galatians 4:27
Isaiah 54:13	John 6:45
Isaiah 55:3	Acts 13:34
Isaiah 56:7	Mark 11:17a
Isaiah 59:7–8	Romans 3:15–17
Isaiah 59:20–21	Romans 11:26–27
Isaiah 61:1–2	Luke 4:18–19
Isaiah 64:4	1 Corinthians 2:9
Isaiah 65:1–2	Romans 10:20–21
Isaiah 66:1–2	Acts 7:49–50
Isaiah 66:24	Mark 9:48

Jeremiah 7:11	Mark 11:17b
Jeremiah 9:24	1 Corinthians 1:31
Jeremiah 9:24	2 Corinthians 10:17
Jeremiah 31:15	Matthew 2:18
Jeremiah 31:31–34	Hebrews 8:8–12
Jeremiah 31:33–34	Romans 11:27
Daniel 7:13	Revelations 1:13
Daniel 9:27	Mark 13:14
Hosea 1:10	Romans 9:26
Hosea 2:23	Romans 9:25
Hosea 6:6	Matthew 9:13
Hosea 10:8	Luke 23:30
Hosea 11:1	Matthew 2:15
Hosea 13:14	1 Corinthians 15:55
Hosea 14:2	Hebrews 13:15
Joel 2:28–32	Acts 2:17–21
Joel 2:32	Romans 10:13
Amos 5:25–27	Acts 7:42–43
Amos 9:11–12	Acts 15:16–17
Micah 5:2	Matthew 2:6
Micah 7:6	Matthew 10:35–36
Habakkuk 1:5	Acts 13:41
Habakkuk 2:3–4	Hebrews 10:37–38
Habakkuk 2:4	Romans 1:17
Habakkuk 2:4	Galatians 3:11
Haggai 2:6	Hebrews 12:26
Zechariah 9:9	Matthew 21:5
Zechariah 9:9	John 12:15
Zechariah 11:12–13	Matthew 27:9–10
Zechariah 12:10	John 19:37
Zechariah 13:7	Mark 14:27
Malachi 1:2–3	Romans 9:13
Malachi 3:1	Mark 1:2

APPENDIX B:

FUNDAMENTALS OF BIBLE STUDY

1. BASIC BIBLE STUDY LIBRARY

This book has benefited from *How to Read the Bible for All Its Worth*, written by Gordon Fee and Douglas Stuart in 1982 and most recently revised 2003. They used the standard methods of Bible study with added emphasis on the type of literary form (or genre). The book is highly recommended in preparation for (and during) Bible study. Also useful is R. C. Sproul's *Knowing Scripture*, published in 1977.

Books recommended for this basic library for Bible study — including the Bibles — not only have integrity but are also in print and affordable. Begin with a recent but scholarly translation of the Bible. Consult Fee and Stuart if the choice is difficult. Do not use a freely-translated or paraphrased version of the Bible. Among the very best scholarly versions available for Protestants is the NIV study version (or for Catholics the 'New American Bible'). In addition to the all-important study Bible, keep these three basic tools at hand:

1. *Eerdman's Handbook to the Bible*.
2. *Nelson's New Illustrated Bible Dictionary*.
3. One or two volume references like *The New International Bible Commentary* or *Evangelical Commentary on the Bible*.

The choices shown above for these three tools are not the only acceptable ones. There are many. Get what is highly recommended and affordable. Also available and affordable are The NIV Study Bible software programs by Zondervan for the home computer. Versions of the software that also include dictionaries and commentaries may be real bargains.

Many other aids are available: *Animals of Bible Lands*, *Plants of the Bible*, *New Manners and Customs of Bible Times* and other more narrowly focused help-books. Add these later if the interest justifies them. A word of caution is necessary about commentaries and other aids. Consult these supports last if possible. There is a danger of reading only supports.

2. BASIC BIBLE METHODOLOGY

In their book Fee and Stuart point out that the scholars are usually interested in what the biblical text meant to the people contemporary with the writing. This focus is often called exegesis. On the other hand the Christian readers of today are usually interested in what the biblical text means to them in the present. This focus is often called hermeneutics. However the interest in this book is also in what the Biblical text meant to Jesus and his followers. To those initiating Bible study of the Old Testament this focus on Jesus and his followers should also be of interest. Attempt to understand Bible text at three levels: the original meaning, the meaning to Jesus and his followers and the meaning to today's Christian. These are three daunting tasks.

The first step in Bible study is exegesis. Even within exegesis there are two major questions to ask about a passage. The first major question is 'What does the passage mean within the framework of the entire book or the context?' What is the historical setting? Is it a time of peace? Or tribulation? What does the 'genre' or literary form of the context suggest? Is it straight historical narrative? Is it prophetic literature? Is it a psalm? If so, what kind? Fee and Stuart emphasize that each literary form offers unique challenges. Here are the literary forms Fee and Stuart have analyzed in their book for differing approaches to the Old Testament:

1. Old Testament law.
2. Old Testament prophets
3. Old Testament psalms.
4. Old Testament narratives.
5. Old Testament wisdom literature.

To continue with the first major question in exegesis, what was the purpose of the passage? The study Bible itself offers much information on this kind of question. The second major question in exegesis is about content. What do the words in the specific passage mean? This is not always obvious, especially in the letters of Paul. Don't seek outside help too soon. Wrestle with the passage. Remember exegesis is trying to understand what the writer was saying at the time.

The second step in Bible study is hermeneutics (some scholars include exegesis within hermeneutics, so these are not precisely defined words). Normally the last step is to interpret the meaning of the passage for the present time—for Christians of today. In a sense when Jesus and his followers quoted the Old Testament they were taking these steps. They well understood the meaning the Old Testament writer intended for a passage, but they had their own interpretation of what the passage meant for them.

Remember not to reverse the process. It can be misleading to leap to conclusions about the present-day meaning, here called 'step two', without examining the meanings of the past, which should have been 'step one'. Deciphering the original meaning is always the first step. The entire process of Bible study, especially for a three-level interpretation, is demanding. That is why one needs ample time to study the key Old Testament books like Genesis, Isaiah and the Psalms. That is why one can not apply this three-level approach to every book in the Old Testament. Time constraints make that an impossible task for a lay person. But study and enjoy 'the Bible Jesus loved'!

REFERENCES CITED

Aageson, James W., "Written also for our sake: Paul's use of scripture in the four major epistles, with a study of 1 Corinthians 10", 152-181, in Stanley E. Porter, editor, *Hearing the Old Testament in the New Testament* (Grand Rapids, Michigan: Wm. B. Eerdmans, 2006).

Alexander, David and Pat, editors, *Eerdmans Handbook to the Bible* (Grand Rapids, Michigan: Wm. B. Eerdmans, 1983.

Archer, Gleason and Gregory Chirichigno, *Old Testament Quotations in the New Testament* (Chicago: Moody Press, 1983).

Beale, G. K. and D. A. Carson, editors, *Commentary on the New Testament Use of the Old Testament* (Baker Academic, 2007).

Berding, Kenneth and Jonathan Lunde, editors, *Three Views on the New Testament Use of the Old Testament* (Grand Rapids, Michigan: Zondervan, 2008).

Bratcher, Robert G., editor, *Old Testament Quotations in the New Testament*, 3rd ed. (New York: United Bible Societies, 1987).

Bruce, F. F., *The Canon of Scripture* (Downers Grove, Illinois: Inter-Varsity Press, 1988).

—, *The New Testament Development of Old Testament Themes* (UK: Paternoster Press, 1968, reprinted by Wm. B. Eerdmans, 1969).

—, *The Spreading Flame* (UK: Paternoster Press, 1958, reprinted by Wm. B. Eerdmans, 1995).

—, editor, *The New International Bible Commentary* (Grand Rapids, Michigan: Zondervan, 1999 revision).

Cansdale, George S.. *Animals of Bible Lands* (UK: Paternoster Press, 1970).

Davies, W. D., *Invitation to the New Testament* (New York: Doubleday, 1966).

Edersheim, Alfred, *The Life and Times of Jesus the Messiah* (UK: 1883, reprinted many times).

Elwell, Walter A., editor, *Evangelical Commentary on the Bible* (Grand Rapids, Michigan: Baker Book House, 1989).

Eusebius. *De Praeparatio Evangelica* (A Preparation for the Gospel). Book 8. 4th Century AD.

Fee, Gordon and Douglas Stuart, *How to Read the Bible for All Its Worth*, 3rd ed. (Grand Rapids: Zondervan, 2003).

Gower, Ralph, *New Manners and Customs of Bible Times* (Chicago: Moody Press, 2000 revision of Fred Wight, 1953).

International Bible Society, *The Holy Bible, New International Version* (North American Edition). (Grand Rapids, Michigan: Zondervan, 1984).

Kidner, Derek, *Genesis: an Introduction & Commentary* (Downers Grove, Illinois: InterVarsity Press, 1967).

—, *Psalms 1–72: an Introduction & Commentary* (Downers Grove, Illinois: InterVarsity Press, 1973).

—, *Psalms 73–150: an Introduction & Commentary* (Downers Grove, Illinois: InterVarsity Press, 1973).

Lewis, C. S., *Reflections on the Psalms* (New York: Harcourt Brace Jovanovich, 1958).

Lockyer, Herbert, Sr., general editor. *Nelson's Illustrated Bible Dictionary* (Nashville: Thomas Nelson Publishers, 1986).

Moldenke, Harold N. and Alma L., *Plants of the Bible* (Mineola, NY: Dover Publications, 1986).

Nave, Orville J., *Nave's Topical Bible* (Peabody, Massachusetts: Hendrickson Publishers, 1997).

New, David S., *Old Testament Quotations in the Synoptic Gospels, and the Two-Document Hypothesis* (Atlanta, Georgia: Scholars Press, 1993)

Nicole, Roger, "The New Testament Use of the Old Testament", 135-151, in *Revelation and the Bible,* ed. Carl F. H. Henry (Grand Rapids: Baker, 1958).

Packer, James, Merrill Tenney and William White, Jr., *The Bible Almanac* (Nashville: Thomas Nelson Publishers, 1980).

Sandra L. Richter, *The Epic of Eden: A Christian Entry into the Old Testament* (IVP Academic, 2008).

Schaeffer, Francis A., *Genesis in Space and Time* (Downers Grove: InterVarsity Press, 1972).

Schroeder, Gerald, *Genesis and the Big Bang* (New York: Bantam Doubleday Dell Publishers, 1990).

Shanks, Herschel, James C. VanderKam, P. Kyle McCarter, Jr. and James A. Sanders, *The Dead Sea Scrolls After Forty Years* (Washington, DC: Biblical Archaeology Society, 1992).

Sproul, R. C., *Knowing Scripture* (Downers Grove, Illinois: InterVarsity Press, 1977).

Vine, W. E., *Isaiah: Prophecies, Promises, Warnings* (UK: Oliphants Ltd., 1946).

Walvoord, John F., *The Prophecy Knowledge Handbook* (Wheaton, Illinois: Victor Books, 1990).

Wenham, John, *Christ and the Bible*, 3rd edition (Downers Grove, Illinois: InterVarsity Press, 1994).

Young, Edward J., *The Book of Isaiah,* 3 vols. (Grand Rapids, Michigan: Wm. B. Eerdmans, 1965).

END NOTES

[1] All Scriptural quotations, unless otherwise noted, are taken from the HOLY BIBLE, NEW INTERNATIONAL VERSION®, NIV® Copyright © 1973, 1978, 1984 by Biblica, Inc.™ Used by permission. All rights reserved worldwide.

[2] G. K. Beale and D. A. Carson, editors, *Commentary on the New Testament Use of the Old Testament* (Baker Academic, 2007), xxvi, emphasize the "astonishing variety of ways in which the various NT authors make reference to the OT".

[3] Roger Nicole, "The New Testament Use of the Old Testament," in *Revelation and the Bible,* ed. Carl F. H. Henry (Grand Rapids: Baker, 1958), 135-51.

[4] F. F. Bruce, *The Canon of Scripture* (Downers Grove, Illinois: InterVarsity Press, 1988), page 180.

[5] quoted in F. F. Bruce, *The Canon of Scripture,* 1988, 23.

[6] Take those same Jewish Holy Scriptures and do the following: 1. Keep Ruth and Lamentations separate. 2. Count each of the 'Twelve' separately. 3. Divide each of Samuel, Kings, Chronicles and Ezra-Nehemiah into two books. What is the result? The 39 books of the Protestant Old Testament.

[7] On the other hand, some books that are accepted as holy by both Catholics and Protestants are not mentioned either. But as stated earlier the canonicity of the Apocrypha is beyond the scope of this investigation.

[8] This oral law was codified as the 'Mishana', the first part of the Jewish Talmud, after the time of Jesus.

[9] Gleason Archer and Gregory Chirichigno, *Old Testament Quotations in the New Testament* (Chicago: Moody Press, 1983). Archer and Chirichigno discerned six categories, some of which are distinguished by very subtle differences. A significant conclusion by Archer and Chirichigno was that less than 10 percent of the quotations appeared to be directly drawn from the Hebrew of the Masoretic Text. The rest were from the Septuagint, even though presumably it was translated from the Masoretic text or an older Hebrew text.

[10] John Wenham, *Christ and the Bible,* 3rd edition (Downers Grove, Illinois: InterVarsity Press, 1994), page 100.

---

[11] Kenneth Berding and Jonathan Lunde, editors, *Three Views on the New Testament Use of the Old Testament* (Zondervan, 2008), discuss the complexities of how quotations were used. Even their debate is limited. There is an ever expanding literature on the subject.

[12] W. D. Davies, *Invitation to the New Testament* (New York: Doubleday, 1966), 12. Quotations of the Old Testament in the New Testament firmly prove the new covenant in Christ sprang from the old covenants. In fact, the new covenant was inevitable.

[13] Q is from 'Quelle', which means 'source' in German. Among many, David S. New, *Old Testament Quotations in the Synoptic Gospels, and the Two-Document Hypothesis* (Atlanta: Scholars Press, 1993), elaborates on the two-document (Mark and Q) hypothesis.

[14] Yet another twist is that Deuteronomy 17:7 is repeated five times within Deuteronomy itself. This however does not affect the numbers under consideration.

[15] Here is another subject too large for the scope of this book. Just which letters were actually Paul's has long been debated. This book assumes Paul's letters included all 11 books from Romans through 2 Timothy. This issue is marginal at best. The books most in dispute — the letters to Titus and Timothy — account for a mere two percent of the quotations attributed to Paul's letters.

[16] Jesus however referred to Daniel as a 'prophet'. Bible students of today also consider Daniel a prophet. But in the Jewish Holy Scriptures the book of Daniel was in the 'Writings'.

[17] John Wenham, *Christ and the Bible*, 1994, 17–21. Wenham argues convincingly that Jesus considered events in the Old Testament factual. On pages 91–97, Wenham reached the same conclusion regarding Paul and the other New Testament writers. See also Francis A. Schaeffer, *Genesis in Space and Time* (Downers Grove: InterVarsity Press, 1972) for convincing arguments that Jesus and his followers accepted even the very earliest Bible figures Adam and Eve as factual, not symbolic.

[18] James W. Aageson, "Written also for our sake: Paul's use of scripture in the four major epistles, with a study of 1 Corinthians 10", 152-181 in Stanley E. Porter, Editor, *Hearing the Old Testament in the New Testament* (Wm. B. Eerdmans, 2006), looks at the use another way: Most of the explicit quotations, about 90, are concentrated in the four major epistles (Romans, Corinthians and Galatians). This writer tallies 94: counting 56 in Romans, 17 in 1 Corinthians, 11 in 2 Corinthians and 10 in Galatians.

[19] Although discerning the sources of direct quotations is beyond the scope of this book, note the following affinity with the Septuagint (Greek Old Testament) determined by the United Bible Societies' investigation (Robert G. Bratcher, editor, *Old Testament Quotations in the New Testament*, 1987):

Jesus.	13 of 41, or 32 percent.
Paul.	59 of 108, or 55 percent.
Other followers of Jesus.	48 of 98, or 49 percent.

In comparison to this study headed by Bratcher, the previously cited 1983 study of Archer and Chirichigno attributed more quotes to the Septuagint as the source.

[20] According to John Wenham, *Christ and the Bible*, 1994, 136 and 208, Philo's quote is preserved only in Eusebius, *De Praeparatio Evangelica* (A Preparation for the Gospel), 4th Century AD, Book 8 (of 15).

[21] Derek Kidner, *Genesis: an Introduction & Commentary* (Downers Grove, Illinois: InterVarsity Press, 1967), 14.

[22] Gerald Schroeder, *Genesis and the Big Bang* (New York: Bantam Doubleday Dell Publishers, 1990). His reconciliation seems logical although very difficult to grasp.

[23] Exodus 23:19, Exodus 34:26 and Deuteronomy 14:21.

[24] James Packer, Merrill Tenney and William White, Jr., *The Bible Almanac* (Nashville: Thomas Nelson Publishers, 1980), 110. These ancient peoples included Hittites, Persians, Canaanites, Greeks, and Romans.

[25] The Egyptian pharaoh Akhnaton advocated the worship of one god—the sun god Aton. But Akhnaton's reign was short-lived (1375–1366 BC) and his advocacy of Aton unpopular among his own Egyptians. So it can not be truthfully said that the Egyptian civilization ever worshipped only one god.

[26] Later than the time of Moses Jews began to believe that after death they continued to exist in a shadowy 'Sheol', not that such a dismal prospect would have been much comfort.

[27] John F. Walvoord, *The Prophecy Knowledge Handbook* (Wheaton, Illinois: Victor Books, 1990), 648-654, lists all the prophecies of the Pentateuch, with Messianic prophecies indicated.

[28] Mark 12:29–31 is cited by some believers as the message of the New Testament. It is not. *It is the message of the Old Testament*. It is the essence of the Law. No law can improve on the Old Testament Law of Moses but the message of the New Testament is not the Law. Jesus himself made it very clear in Luke 16:16: "The Law and the Prophets were proclaimed until John. Since that time, the good news of the

---

kingdom of God is being preached..."

29 Steve Moyise, *Paul and Scripture: Studying the New Testament Use of the Old Testament* (Baker Academic, 2010) discusses Paul's differing views on the authority of the Law (Pentateuch) and whether they can be reconciled.

30 John Wenham, *Christ and the Bible*, 1994, 92.

31 Honed by his earlier rabbinical training. The technique of stringing together a succession of quotes from Scripture was called 'charaz' (Hebrew for string of pearls'). See Alfred Edersheim, *The Life and Times of Jesus the Messiah*, Vol. 1: The Ascent, chapter 10 (UK: 1883, reprinted many times).

32 Genesis 15:6 is the same passage Paul quoted in Romans 4:3 to assert in Romans 5:1 that "we have been justified through faith". This seeming contradiction between Paul's faith alone and James' faith in conjunction with good works is one of few among the New Testament writers. It is reassuring that the custodians of Christianity 'doctored' neither Romans nor the book of James to remove what appears to be disagreement.

33 This is ambiguous in that the psalm may have been written by David or for David.

34 In contrast, the captivity and exile of Jews at the hands of the Babylonians was a time of turmoil but not a time of triumph.

35 It seems liberal scholarship attempts to move the authorship of Old Testament texts to as late a time as possible. The result is to discount all prophecy as after-the-fact chicanery.

36 Gordon Fee and Douglas Stuart, *How to Read the Bible for All Its Worth* (Grand Rapids, Michigan: Zondervan Pub., 1993), 194–197.

37 Derek Kidner, *Psalms 1–72: an Introduction & Commentary* (Downers Grove, Illinois: InterVarsity Press, 1973), 60.

38 Derek Kidner, *Psalms 1–72: an Introduction & Commentary*, 1973, 18–25, and *Psalms 73–150: an Introduction & Commentary* (Downers Grove, Illinois: InterVarsity Press, 1973), 350, lists as Messianic Psalms 2, 22, 35, 40, 41, 45, 69, 72, 84, 89, 97, 102, 109, 110 and 118. Jesus and his followers quoted all of them but 72, 84 and 89.

39 John F. Walvoord, *The Prophecy Knowledge Handbook*, 1990. 664-672, lists all the prophecies of the Psalms, indicating Messianic prophecies. Walvoord lists as Messianic all Kidner's Messianic psalms except 40, 45, 84 and 109. In addition Walvoord included psalms 8, 9, 10, 16, 24, 27, 31, 34, 38, 68, 78, 96, 99, 103, 121, 132, 145 and 147. Of

Walvoord's 29 Messianic psalms, 16 were quoted by Jesus and his followers; 13 were not quoted.

[40] David and Pat Alexander, editors, *Eerdmans Handbook to the Bible*. (Grand Rapids, Michigan: Wm. B. Eerdmans Publishing, 1983), 329, lists 11 psalms with 'Christ in the Psalms': 2, 8, 16, 22, 40, 41, 45, 69, 72, 110 and 118. Eerdmans lists such psalms as Messianic only if Jesus and his followers recognized them as Messianic or the word 'Messiah' is used.

[41] Derek Kidner, *Psalms 1–72*, 1973, especially page 24.

[42] C. S. Lewis, *Reflections on the Psalms* (New York: Harcourt Brace Jovanovich, 1958), 1-9. See also Kidner, *Psalms 1–72*, 1973, 1-4, for a discussion of the poetry.

[43] On the other hand, don't underestimate the profundity of Psalms. F. F. Bruce, *The New Testament Development of Old Testament Themes* (UK: Paternoster Press, 1968, reprinted by Wm. B. Eerdmans Publishing, 1969). 18, notes G. W. Anderson claimed if scholars knew only the Psalms (and no other Old Testament books), they would still possess all the themes of Old Testament theology.

[44] In verse 7 of Romans 3 Paul went on to write, "To those who by persistence in doing good seek glory, honor and immortality, he will give eternal life." Did Paul say here that 'doing good' earns eternal life, contradicting 'justification is by faith alone' advanced by him so many times?

[45] All six however are considered Messianic by John F. Walvoord, *The Prophecy Knowledge Handbook*, 1990, 664–672

[46] The northern kingdom was also called 'Israel'. Yet *all* the descendants of Jacob are Israelites. If the northern kingdom is called 'Ephraim', much confusion is avoided. So this book never restricts the meaning of Israel to the northern kingdom.

[47] It is noteworthy that 'the light of life' occurs in both the Greek Septuagint and the Hebrew Dead Sea scrolls — but in the Masoretic Hebrew text there is no object for 'he will see'...

[48] Among the rich offerings not to be ignored in chapters 60 through 66 is Isaiah's (especially 66:3) condemnation of animal sacrifice.

[49] John F. Walvoord, *The Prophecy Knowledge Handbook*, 1990, 672–681, enumerated 31 Messianic prophecies in all of Isaiah. Chapters 40 to 66, the 'book of comfort', contain 22 of those 31.

[50] There is also evidence that Joel and Obadiah were contemporaries of Nahum, Habakkuk and Zephaniah.

[51] This is another example (the other, Isaiah 66:3) of God 'repealing' the old laws of animal sacrifice and burnt offerings.

[52] So much for the often repeated fallacy that nowhere in the Old Testament is hope offered for an afterlife. Also, consider this quote from Daniel 12:2, "Multitudes who sleep in the dust of the earth will awake: some to everlasting life..."

[53] Jeremiah precedes Zechariah in time. The Matthew quote can be pieced together from Jeremiah 19:1-3 and 32:6-9 with some effort.

[54] Isaiah 6:6–7 depicted a live coal used to burn away sin.

[55] John F. Walvoord, *The Prophecy Knowledge Handbook*, 1990, 70. Esther is unique in another way. It is the only book of the Protestant Old Testament not found among the Hebrew Dead Sea scrolls (see F. F. Bruce, *The Canon of Scripture*, 1988, 39). Especially compelling from the viewpoint of this book — *The Bible Jesus Loved* — is the fact that the five most common Dead Sea scrolls are Genesis (15), Exodus (15), Deuteronomy (25), Psalms (30), and Isaiah (19)! See also Herschel Shanks et al., *The Dead Sea Scrolls After Forty Years*, 1992, 29.

[56] Gordon Fee and Douglas Stuart, *How to Read the Bible for All Its Worth*, 1993, 213.

[57] C. S. Lewis, *Reflections on the Psalms*, 1958, 114-115.

[58] It is not included in the tally for Paul of quotations from Psalms. To eliminate duplication in the tallies, the former prophets received precedence over the Psalms.

[59] John F. Walvoord, *The Prophecy Knowledge Handbook*, 1990, 697.

[60] Sandra L. Richter, *The Epic of Eden: A Christian Entry into the Old Testament* (IVP Academic, 2008), 17-20.

[61] Genesis 3:15; 9:25–27; 12:3; 17:15–19; 22:15–18; 26:4; 28:14; 49:10–12 in John Walvoord, *The Prophecy Knowledge Handbook*, 1990, 648–651.

www.ingramcontent.com/pod-product-compliance
Lightning Source LLC
Chambersburg PA
CBHW061740020426
42331CB00006B/1303